Maine's Waterfalls

A Comprehensive Guide

Patricia Hughes

177 Waterfalls That Shaped
Maine's Wet and Wild History

Schiffer
Publishing Ltd

4880 Lower Valley Road, Atglen, PA 19310

Dedication

There are so many people who have supported me throughout the years. All my family and friends deserve to be mentioned here, and I appreciate them all. *Thank you* just does not seem to be enough to say, but the words are sincerely meant for everyone. Mom, Dad, B.J., Brenda, Michael, Nicolette, Madeline, Roxanne, David, John, Michael K., Auntie and Uncle Jerry, are just the tip of the vast network of people who have supported and helped me with the writing of this book.

Schiffer Books are available at special discounts for bulk purchases for sales promotions or premiums. Special editions, including personalized covers, corporate imprints, and excerpts can be created in large quantities for special needs. For more information contact the publisher:

Published by Schiffer Publishing Ltd.
4880 Lower Valley Road
Atglen, PA 19310
Phone: (610) 593-1777; Fax: (610) 593-2002
E-mail: Info@schifferbooks.com

For the largest selection of fine reference books on this and related subjects, please visit our web site at **www.schifferbooks.com**
We are always looking for people to write books on new and related subjects. If you have an idea for a book please contact us at the above address.

This book may be purchased from the publisher.
Include $5.00 for shipping.
Please try your bookstore first.
You may write for a free catalog.

In Europe, Schiffer books are distributed by
Bushwood Books
6 Marksbury Ave.
Kew Gardens
Surrey TW9 4JF England
Phone: 44 (0) 20 8392 8585; Fax: 44 (0) 20 8392 9876
E-mail: info@bushwoodbooks.co.uk
Website: www.bushwoodbooks.co.uk

Designed by John P. Cheek
Cover design by Bruce Waters
Type set in Friz Quadrata/NewBskvll BT

ISBN: 978-0-7643-3113-8
Printed in China

Unless otherwise noted, photographs by the author.
Compass © James Steidl. Screw Auger Falls, Maine © Paula Stephens. Maine Waterfall © Dave Horgan. Waterfall_camden Maine © Alan Robinson. Gorge © John Anderson. Foot Bridge © Curtis Adams. Water Falls © Curtis Adams. Moxie Falls © Jeff DeVries. These photos courtesy of bigstockphotos.com.

Cover photo: Moxie Falls©Jeff DeVries. Image from BigStockPhoto.com
Page 191: Camden Maine Waterfall. Camden has three waterfalls within the town limits. The parks in town, where waterfalls are the centerpieces, were designed in the late 1920s by the Olmstead Brothers.

Contents

CHAPTER ONE
Introduction

When Waterfalls Ruled!

Since the beginning of time, nature has always been a source of awe, inspiration, and even terror to humans. We have worshiped the force of nature and are awed by the beauty, creative ability, and utter destruction that nature can produce. This is very true in Maine, where the forests seemed to extend forever and the clear rushing water was the only way through the dense woods.

The key to understanding Maine and the way of life that has existed since the state was first created, is to understand and appreciate the water of the land. Rivers, lakes, streams, bogs, and the ocean are the driving force that has created Maine's history. Learning how the water phenomena in the state is (and always was) used, is an exciting journey through Maine's wet and wild history.

Waterfalls are truly magical entities. The sheer volume of water, the thunderous sound, and the immense obstacles are overwhelming when first observed. This water phenomenon staggers the mind of the observer, and it is really no wonder that these are considered spiritual and enchanting places of wonder. It is not so strange that so many natural, spiritual, historical, and even magical events have occurred at these sites. People have been drawn to the power of these places since prehistoric times. There is a theory in the paranormal world that running water may increase supernatural activity. This may explain why some waterfalls are haunted today. They are also dangerous and people have died in them.

At first, the falls were seen as obstacles to get around with carries and portages. Next, they were seen as obstacles to be removed, during the log-driving era. Now, they are seen as objects to be admired and revered with the beginning of tourism in Maine. Though these locations are mere moments in geologic time, they will ultimately transform the cultures that are lucky to have them within their boundaries.

Maine is a swift whirling vortex of water hydraulics. During the last ice age, the sheets of ice moved in a southeasterly direction. When they retreated, they left debris, which blocked valleys and dammed rivers naturally. There is evidence that, before the Ice Age, the Androscoggin River ran north to south, but today the glacial deposits prevent that. Now, the same river runs east, then turns south. The glaciers followed the river valleys making them deeper and wider. After the glaciers retreated, the river just followed the easiest course through the land. Many river rapids were created because the water flowed over glacial debris. Waterfalls were formed when the glacier transformed the landscape, by taking out huge pieces of rock that left ledges and drops for water to fall over.

As an interesting side note, rivers acquire a path through the ground because small curves create faster currents on the outer edge, and erosion carves the outer edge. This causes the river to bend. Nature is very logical, even when perceived as unpredict-able. Too much of a curve and the river becomes a circle or lake, eventually. As strange as it may seem, all rivers tend to double back on themselves, and the average circles that are created have the value of Pi (or 3.14). According to Simon Singh, in the 1998 book *Fermat's Enigma*, this value varies from river to river, so it appears that Pi is "the result of a battle between order and chaos." Rivers that flow across gentle sloping terrain are the ones to be an exact ratio to Pi, however when water is too fast or too steep, the ratio of Pi disappears. So, it could be argued that waterfalls can change the laws of nature to some degree. No wonder we are drawn to these places.

Waterfalls would seem to be easy to describe. They are a section of a river or stream that slides vertically in some way. But it is the details and variations of that description that make these natural wonders so diverse and exciting to behold. Rivers have been, and always will be, vital to the Maine way of life. Virtually all Maine towns were born next to the waterfalls on our magnificent rivers. It was the only transporta-tion system for Native Americans and early settlers. It was the lifeblood of Maine's economy with the logging, trapping, fishing, hunting, and, now, eco-tourism, and river recreation trades. Most mills were built over the falls where Native Americans fished for thousands of years. Land was sold and valued solely based on where falls were located during the settlements of the estates.

Though Maine rivers are relatively young, at least as far as ge-ology is concerned, there is a natural aging process for all rivers. As the river grows old, it becomes less steep and the water moves much slower. The channel will widen into a U-shape. The waterfalls and rapids will eventually disappear from the Maine rivers. These inspiring waterfalls are just a moment in time, and will someday disappear forever.

To understand the violent water phenomena in Maine, a quick lesson in geology is needed. A mile or more of ice covered most of Maine until about 10,000 years ago. That makes the hydraulic features of the state quite young to geologists. Maine waterfalls occur because, as the glacier retreated and melted, the rivers coursed wherever the disrupted terrain allowed. It was inevitable that rivers would encounter the uneven terrain, and that would ultimately cause the development of waterfalls.

The other geological feature unique to Maine is that it is not really part of the North American continent. In the Devonian age, about 360 million years ago, the fabric of this area was about to change dramatically. This event happened due to the theory of plate tectonics. According to this theory, the crust of earth consists of a small number of large, semi-rigid plates all in motion to each other. At various times, these plates are moving around, and sometimes completely change direction. At one time, they actually came together as one continent, surrounded by oceans; then they split apart again with oceans between them. They will eventually all come together again, but not for millions of years.

In the Devonian age, the ancient ocean was called Iapetus, broadly defined as a predecessor of the Atlantic Ocean. This ocean had many scattered micro-plates in it. The eastern line of the North American continent ended at Vermont. The micro-continent of Avalonia slammed into this land mass and accreted, or joined, North America. This formed the state of Maine. It also may be one of the reasons that there are many gem stones found in Oxford County. This was a very violent, thermal event, and it probably caused quite a bit of rock to melt. This is considered the event that caused the major folding of the rocks that are seen in the Appalachian Mountain chain today. So, between the depression of the land because of the glaciers, and the bump and crunch of two continents, wild water channels were created in Maine.

The only way to travel on these turbulent waterways was by birch bark canoe. These canoes could be carried by hand, when necessary, at portage sites around waterfalls, and could be poled upstream through sections too shallow and swift to paddle. Birch bark canoes were said to be invented in Maine by the Native Americans, but regardless of whether that is true or not, evidence shows that this type of boat was used 4,000 years ago in this area.

The Native Americans lived on the coast of Maine most of the time. The Native Americans would name the water phenomena, as they were traveling upstream. For example the Native American words, *nesowadnehunk,* means " river runs through mountain," *sededunkchunk,* means "rapids at the mouth," and *madunkehunk,* means "height of land stream." The Native Americans who lived in Maine were part of the Algonquian branch of the Algonquian-Wakashan linguistic stock. The proper name of the tribe is Wabanaki, a word that refers to morning and in the east. The French shortened the name to Abnaki or Abenaki. (In this book, the references to the tribe will be Abenaki.)

The falls in Maine are usually found away from the coastline in the northeast region of the state. They form near the White Mountains on the Maine and New Hampshire border. The falls near the coast are reversing falls, which are tidal phenomenon, but are not technically falls. The reversing falls occur when rocks are situated in a narrow passage of tidal water where the volume and height of the current reaching the passage is significant. When the tidal current strikes the rocks, it tumbles over them to a lower level of land. As the water on both sides of the rocks become equal, there are no falls at all. Then, the tide reverses, and eventually the difference in water level again becomes significant forming the falls in the opposite direction. This book will discuss all the types of the natural and man-made falls, also known as dams, that are found in the state, including these reversing falls.

There are three reasons why are there so many waterfalls in Maine. One reason is that there is a mass of mountains that lie closer to the coastline geographically, than occur anywhere else along the eastern seaboard. That may happen because Maine was not part of the original eastern seaboard. The second reason is that Maine does not lack for adequate rainfall. The third is that the geology of Maine provides great conditions for the origin of waterfalls. To create a waterfall, the flowing water must find varying degrees of resistance to erosion in the rock. The soft parts of the land erode easily, while the harder layers remain intact, so while the land tries to resist the water, waterfalls are created.

What actually constitutes a waterfall is not just the height of a fall, but also the volume of water flowing over the falls. To complicate matters more, the height of a waterfall is subject to interpretations. A waterfall usually starts with a series of rapids, then goes over a vertical or somewhat vertical drop, and ends with a cataract over debris at the bottom. Hydraulic erosion, river or stream bottom content, landslides or glacial debris usually cause the rubble at the bottom of the waterfall, which causes rapids.

With the passage of time, a waterfall must either migrate upstream, or serve as the reason for the down cutting along the reach of the river. The question may arise as to why a book about waterfalls also explores whitewater phenomena. The reason is really simple. The rapid is the first and last part of the life of a waterfall.

Maine Waterfall Types and Terms

Man-Made Waterfalls—Also Known as Dams

Dams in Maine were usually built for three reasons. The first reason was to harness the incredible power that these fast and wild rivers could provide to run the mills that were built along the riverbanks. The second was to create electricity for the surrounding areas. The third is because of the log-driving industry. Not all dams were built over rapids or fall sites. Dams were built in the logging era to overcome an obstacle on the river. That could mean anything, including low water levels, swamps, dead water, or a rapid or fall. Some of these dams were built with dirt, logs, and any other material that was readily available. Some were always meant to be temporary and have been breached, while others, made of stone or concrete, were built to stand the test of time.

There were so many dams built on Maine rivers, that many of the names have been lost in time. Numerous dams that existed, or that still exist, have been documented in the book, but many have never been recorded, especially the temporary dams, so they are not included here. Various dams were called the "new dam" or the "old dam" and were located on the same river. Sometimes a beaver would even build a dam!

Without a specific description or location, it is impossible to record when or where some dams were built. There are reasons why some dams have been recorded here. One reason encompasses why a dam was built; there must have been fast moving water in that area. Some of the dams were built over rapid water that may not have had a specific name, so the name of the dam is used as the name of the fast water. This may be the only way to document the site. Another reason is that the dam has historical significance.

There are, and were, so many dams—over 1,000 at one time—because the quick water was so readily available all over the state. It is also important to note how some of the dams today are being removed from the rivers. This is part of the present and future of Maine's water phenomena. This is an ongoing process, an event in the life of a waterfall, forever changing, and never complete.

Block or River Waterfalls

These falls are usually found on a river. They are typically wider than tall, and have a high volume of water.

Curtain or Stream Waterfalls

Found on a mountain stream, these waterfalls are usually taller than wide. The water flow is either small or medium.

Cascading Waterfalls

These are waterfalls that are formed by water descending over gradually-sloping rocks, or a series of small steps in quick succession.

Plunge, Cataract, or Ledge Waterfalls

Waterfalls of this nature are formed when a stream flows off the edge of a cliff and free-falls to the bottom of the site.

Overhanging Ledge Waterfalls

The overhanging ledge waterfall is usually the most impressive of all waterfalls and is formed when the ledge over which the stream flows extends out from the rest of the cliff wall.

Slide Waterfalls

A downward steeply-sloping rock cliff forms these waterfalls. They are very similar to cascading falls.

Parallel or Segmented Waterfalls

These are two waterfalls that fall side-by-side.

Tiered or Multi-Cascading Waterfalls

Tiered or multi-cascading falls cascade down in many tiny parallel cascades or in distinct drops in close succession to each other.

Fan Waterfalls

These falls are created when a narrow cascade spreads out in a fan-like formation at the bottom of a waterfall.

Staircase Waterfalls

This waterfall falls in a single stream over many small edges, creating the image of a staircase. Many of these falls flow over granite bedrock in Maine.

Horsetail Waterfalls

Characterized by the constant or semi-constant contact the water maintains with the bedrock as it falls, these falls slide vertically or gradually.

Punchbowl Waterfalls

Punchbowl waterfalls occur where the stream is constricted to a narrow breadth, and is forcefully shot outward and downward into a large pool.

Combination Waterfalls

These waterfalls include features of more than one type of waterfall. For example, a waterfall could cascade at the top and then plunge off a ledge at the bottom. The majority of waterfalls fall into this category.

Rapids

This water phenomenon occurs when a section of a stream has a current with moderate velocity. Extruding rocks and debris produces whitewater on the surface. They can usually be found before the vertical drop of a waterfall.

Stream

A stream is a constantly moving body of water, confined to the lowest possible depression in the Earth's surface. Running water is a powerful erosion component. Streams can flow year round called perennial streams or intermittent flows, only when volume is high, called intermittent streams.

Waterfalls can be very scenic, and today, some are protected as tourist sites, but this is a very recent development. Another question this book will try to answer is: Why have there been so many historical events that have happened around waterfalls? There are actually a number of reasons. The main one is that until recently, the only real way to travel in Maine was through water. The forests were just too thick to move through at one time. There were animal trails and very narrow, rough footpaths, but the only way to trek a long distance quickly was through the water.

During the log-driving days, rapids and waterfalls were considered hazardous and were very unpopular. Unless the water volume was running high, it usually meant log jams. Many waterfalls were destroyed, or were reduced to what they are today, to ease the passage of logs. That is why so many dams were built, river runners needed to increase the water level and help ease the passage of logs to move along the river.

Fishing was vital, even life sustaining, to the Native Americans on these rivers. The waterfalls were the place where they would catch their food for the coming year. When the Europeans first started to dam the rivers, the food stopped coming to the falls, and the conflicts really started heating up between the Native Americans and the Europeans. Most conflicts occurred in the early years because of the use of waterfalls. The pools beneath the waterfalls were where the fish migrated, and it meant life or death to the tribes in the area. Dams that were built by the settlers meant that no fish could migrate.

The main catch was Atlantic Salmon. The Atlantic Salmon is often referred to as the "true salmon," but it is not a salmon; it is a trout. It is closely related to the brown trout. In the past, these fish have been known to grow to 100 pounds. This species has been declining for many years. Maine is the only state that contains wild Atlantic Salmon populations. There are only eight rivers in Maine that still sustain a naturally reproducing salmon population. They are:

Dennys River, East Machias River, Machias River, Pleasant River, Narraguagus River, Ducktrap River, Sheepscot River, and Cove Brook.

Today in Maine, Atlantic Salmon can not be harmed, harassed, pursed, hunted, shot, wounded, killed, trapped, captured, or collected on these rivers.

All sixteen counties in Maine have fast water phenomena, in other words, a falls site. There are many cascades, rips, rapids, dams, and even waterfalls that remain unknown, unnamed, and drowned to this day. Many times the names were misspelled or different names were used for the same falls. I've tried to state the varied names and history of the water phenomena known to the best oral and written documentation that could be found. Water also does not flow according to county lines. There are water phenomena in this book that may go through two or more counties, towns, and even rivers. They are listed in only one county, in one town, and on one river for this text.

Use the key that follows the introduction to gain a sense of visitor features for these wonderful sites. Whether it is to take a fantastic photo, get some hiking exercise, or just learn the history of the waterfalls, this handy guide will point you in the right direction. So, enough with the general explanations! Let us start to find the 177 waterfalls that shaped the state of Maine!

⚠ Visiting these waterfalls can be dangerous and may be located on private property. Though the directions are given in the book, permission must be received by the visitor before going unless the site is located in a state park. The visitor must take care when visiting these places. Deaths have occurred at some of these locations, and therefore, you visit at your own risk. Be cognizant of permissions and safety issues.

Waterfalls Site Legend

This rating system is based on a 1, 2, 3, method and will appear at the end of each waterfall.

1 icon = Low / Poor
2 icons = Medium / Average
3 icons = High / Best

Sites will be rated on:

Accessibility =

Historic Significance =

Photo Opportunity = 📷

All Waterfalls shown here will have at least one 3 rating in one category. Many will have a 3 rating in multiple categories.

For example:
Dear Rips provides a 2 for Accessibility, a 3 for historical significance, and a 1 for photo opportunity.

Maine's Counties

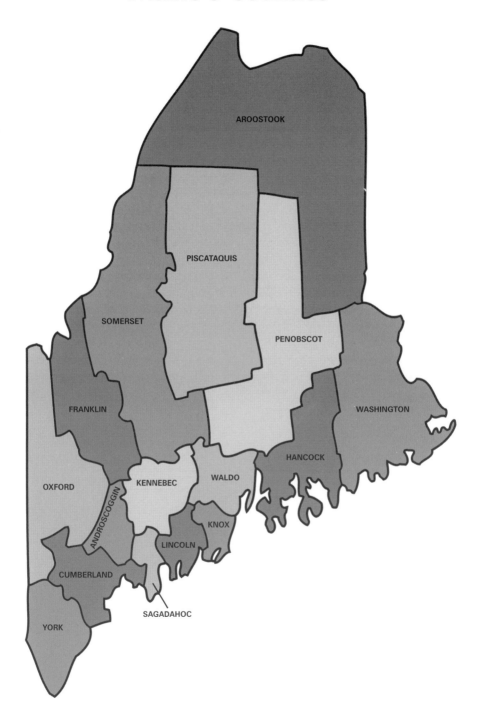

Androscoggin County

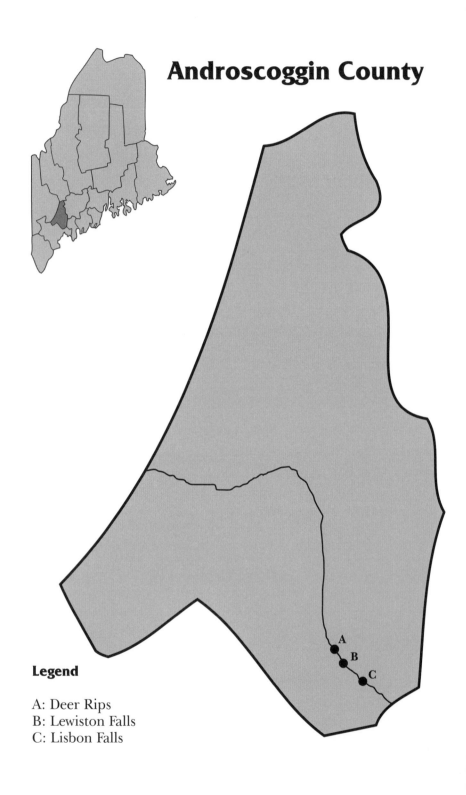

Legend

A: Deer Rips
B: Lewiston Falls
C: Lisbon Falls

CHAPTER TWO
Androscoggin County

The Androscoggin River was originally a fast-flowing river with numerous large falls and long rapids. Most attempts to canal, ferry, supplement, or otherwise adapt the river for transportation failed, because of the number, height, and length of the falls along the river. This river drops 1,500 vertical feet from the Rangeley Lakes to Merrymeeting Bay. Androscoggin is an Abenaki word that means "the place where the fish are cured." There were so many logs driven down this river in 1820, that they were actually counted by the acre, not by the number of logs. Part of this river was so polluted in the logging era that the water was reported to have caught on fire.

In the seventeenth century, a Native American called Pierpole, served the following deposition about the names of falls in this area:

> "I, Pierpole, of lawful age, testify and say that the Indian name of the river was Pejepscook, from Quabacook, what is now called Merrymeeting Bay, up as far as Amitgonpontook, what the English call Harrises falls, and all the river from Harrises Falls up, was called Ammoscongon and the largest falls on the river was above Rockamecook, about twelve miles, and those falls have got three pitches and there is no other falls on the river like them and the Native Americans used to catch the most salmon at the foot of them falls, and the Indians used to say when they went down the river from Rockamecook and when they got down over the falls by Harrises they say now come Pejepscook."

The Native American name for Merrymeeting Bay is *Quabacook*, and the Native American corn planting grounds were at Canton and Jay Points was called Rockamecook, and at one time, the Atlantic Salmon ascended the river as far as Rumford Falls.

Deer Rips
(Also known as Deer Rips Dam)

Directions: I-95 to Exit 109B toward Winthrop. Sharp right onto Switzerland Road. There is about .1 miles between end of driving to location. Use local maps.

These rapids are found on the Androscoggin River in Auburn. There is a legend about a terrible catastrophe that happened here. The tale starts with a Native American girl who was sleeping in a lean-to near Deer Rips. She heard a noise, and woke to see an Abenaki war party in full war paint making a portage around the rips. She thought that they were on their way to massacre the settlement near Lewiston Falls. She hurried down to the river, saw the scout who had gone ahead to light the beacon light above the falls. She clubbed him with an oak branch, about two feet long, tied him up, put out the fire he had started. Then she climbed a pine tree at the base of the falls. She lit the top of the tree, which confused the war party, and they died plunging over the falls.

Though this account is said to be fictional, or at the very least, a stretch of the truth, there is an old news article that was found at the Androscoggin Historical Society that states that the Rockomeko tribe had planned to attack the settlement near the falls in 1688. They did go past Deer Rips and arrived at Lewiston Falls at night. For some unknown reason, the fire was lit below the falls, instead of above the falls and the war party paddled to their deaths.

There is also a story that says that European men were harassing the Native American women of this area, and the men in the tribe decided to take matters into their own hands. They attacked the village near the falls.

What is actually known is that *something* happened here, and that these stories will continue.

Waterfall Ratings

Lewiston Falls

(Also known as: Uppermost and Great Falls of the Androscoggin; West Pitch Great Falls; Harris Falls; 20-mile Falls; Lewiston Falls Dam; Amitgonpontook)

 Directions: I-95 to Exit 80. Take ME 196 W ramp to Lisbon Street. Turn left onto US 202, turn right onto Island Avenue. There is a small turn out to see the fall site.

These once awesome and incredible falls are located on the Androscoggin River between Lewiston and Auburn. This was considered one of the greatest natural water power ever discovered in Maine. It was a thirty-eight-foot natural cascade fall site and the third set of falls on this river. According to folklore, these falls were named because a Native American logger, named Lewis, lived here. Another darker story is that Lewis fell into the falls drunk and then drowned.

When the Native Americans inhabited this area, the entire river was named for each of the seven sections that were separated by seven different major falls. The whole river region was called Amascoggin, which meant "fish country in the spring time" or "lace of fish spearing." The Native American name for these falls was, Amitgonpontook, which meant "he fishes."

When the first Europeans got here, they believed this river was the most powerful in the world. Western rivers were not known at that time. When the Androscoggin was allowed to flow without any restrictions, the river dropped 1,500 feet and flowed for 165 miles. The river was not navigable at that time, due to the numerous waterfalls here, except by birch bark canoe, and only with many portages. The dams have since calmed this river and many falls remain drowned and unknown to this day.

The first record of settlers here is in 1624. It is reported that seventy-five people settled near the Great Falls of the Pejepscot (which is now called the Androscoggin River). In 1690, the English burned the largest Anasagunticook, or Native American, settlement here. In the mid 1700s, a military group searching for the native people, found no one left. The tribe either died or was driven out of the area. All that was left was a great amount of salmon at the bottom of the falls. The last time Atlantic Salmon was seen here was in 1816.

A natural stone dam created a fifty-foot drop, and there was a covered railroad bridge here in 1869 with a deck truss.

These falls are presently dry today, but colonial oral history tells about caves and hiding places behind these rushing waterfalls. Prehistoric fish hooks and rock sinkers have been found. The bedrock type is purplish-gray quartz-mica schist. A ledge of gneiss causes this descent, and the mica-schist that crosses the river diagonally, also extends to the bed of the river above and below the falls. The largest pegmatite mass in the state crosses the riverbed at these falls. Granite-Pegmatites are the rocks where feldspar, quartz, mica, and gem minerals are found. Anytime pegmatites are found, it is possible that gem minerals will also be discovered. Pegmatite is an intrusive igneous rock that is formed by the gradual cooling and solidification of fluids derived from nearby granites and other rocks.

Diopside has been found at this site. Diopside is an important rock-forming mineral. It is also found in iron meteorites. Diopside is the magnesium rich part of a series which hedenbergite is the iron-rich part. The color of this mineral is clear, white, blue, which is only found in Italy, and pale green to yellowish-greenish brown. If the mineral rutile is in this mineral, then the diopside becomes even more valuable. If it is green, the rutile may create a "cat's eye" type of gemstone. If the color is dark, which includes rutile needles, and is aligned correctly, it can create a four-rayed star called star diopside.

The story that started at Deer Rips continues here. Legends state that a terrible catastrophe occurred. In many re-tellings of this legend, a family by the name of Weir, Weare, or Wier is mentioned. It is said that the son, father, or brother came home to find his family murdered and went looking for the Native Americans who killed them.

In another re-telling, the settlers were searching for a lost girl believed to be taken by the Native Americans. They came upon a scout, who'd landed at the bottom of the falls in a canoe. He was gathering material to make a fire which the settlers believed was a beacon to warn the other tribe members as to where the falls were located, so they killed the scout and built the fire. But unfortunately, when the Native Americans came, everyone went over the falls and died, including their captive.

Still another version of the Native American legend tells that two scouts were searching for a woman who was carried away as a captive by the settlers. They found the party at the falls. They were gathering wood to make a fire above the falls to let the other settlers know where they were. The Native Americans killed the settlers, but were terrified that help was coming, so they jumped into the river and died as they plunged over the falls.

It has been suggested that someone may have moved the lights, not realizing why they were there, but it is said that because of this catastrophe, the Abenaki placed a curse on the river, saying that forever after, three Europeans would die in the river every year.

Something certainly happened here, but what exactly did happen will probably never be known.

There are a couple of interesting side notes to think about. First, why would the Native Americans need lights? Their primary means of travel was by canoe. They would know how to read and ride the river in the day or night. They would not attempt to travel at night, if they needed lights to do so. It is known that the Native Americans did like to prove how brave they were, and may have used the lights to show the place where one should pull off to the side and carry the canoe around the falls, but if the Native American young man actually passed the lights that were put there as a warning that the falls were close and he actually survived the falls, he was considered very brave indeed.

There are other fall sites in this book where the Native Americans would prove their bravery. The real question is: Why would a war party do this? It is known that that this pitch is navigable by canoe, but with caution. Lights may have been needed to run this pitch in the dark, at least for the European settlers.

Waterfall Ratings

Lisbon Falls

(Also known as: Little River Falls; Ten Miles Falls; Worumbo Dam; Amirkangun; Dammikkangan Falls; Lisbon Falls Dam)

 Directions: I-95 to exit 103 toward ME 9 Gardiner. Merge onto ME 196N to exit 3 toward Lisbon. End at Lisbon Falls.

These falls are located on the Androscoggin River in Lisbon Falls. Anmecangin is the Native American name for the falls, which means "much fish." The prehistoric Native American vil-

19

lage was called Amereangan. Thomas Purchase settled this area in 1628.

The falls are known as the Little River Falls because, in 1802, the area was called Little River Plantation before being changed to Lisbon Falls. The name Lisbon was given, because it was popular in Maine in the 1800s to name places after foreign locales. This area was named after Lisbon, Portugal.

In 1864, the famous Worumbo Mill at this site created sterling cloths of pure wool. This wool was fine enough for women's gowns. The cloth won several international prizes for the mill. The mill was declared a historical place in 1973, and is registered with the National Registry of Historic Places.

The natural falls were actually two drops, about ninety feet apart, with a total drop of thirty-one feet. The lower falls was a nearly perfect horseshoe-shaped fall, and the upper falls extended straight across the entire river.

Waterfall Ratings

Mechanic Falls

(Also known as: Bog Falls; Marcal Paper Mills; Bog Brook Falls; Mechanic Falls Dam)

Directions: I-95 to exit 75. US 202 toward Poland Springs. Take ME 122 to ME 26 to ME 11 to ME 124. End at Mechanic Falls.

The pitches right in the center of Mechanic Falls is located on the Little Androscoggin River. These are minor pitches, not in excess of three feet each, with a total drop of thirty-seven feet. The town was settled in 1769, and the paper mill was established in 1850. The site is named for the early local industry or "mechanics," who operated and serviced the mills here. The falls were used to create power for the mills when the area was first settled. There was a covered bridge here at an earlier time. It was called Bog Falls, because the largest stream within the town was called Bog Brook. The water quality of Little Androscoggin River is poor, due in part, to all the mills in the area.

There is a legend about this site that says that Chrysoberyl, gray-green crystals, were discovered. The name comes from the Greek word *Chrysos*, meaning golden, and *beryl*, due to the beryllium content in the mineral. Chrysoberyl is a gem crystal that is popular. There are three types. The first type comes in yellow to green to brown; the second is called Cymophane or "cat's eye," and the third type is called Alexandrite, which is very rare and changes color when light hits it. Alexandrite is not abundant in Maine.

There is also a lost quarry where Schorl or black Tourmaline was found. Schorl is the most common of Tourmaline group, and is black in color. Tourmaline crystals are hemimorphic, meaning they have a different shaped top from the bottom of the crystal. It is the only mineral that will form crystals with a clear triangular cross-section. Like quartz, this crystal is also piezoelectric, meaning it requires a charge to be compressed, twisted, or distorted. This provides a transducer effect between electrical and mechanical oscillations.

Microcline has been found here, which is potash feldspar, and potassium. This is a very important industrial mineral. Microcline is a common mineral, but not a well-known one. It has been used as a semi-precious stone, also known as amazonite and perthite. Microcline is a polymorph of other minerals that share the same chemistry, but have different crystal structures. The color is off white, yellow, flesh pink, brown, or green.

Waterfall Ratings

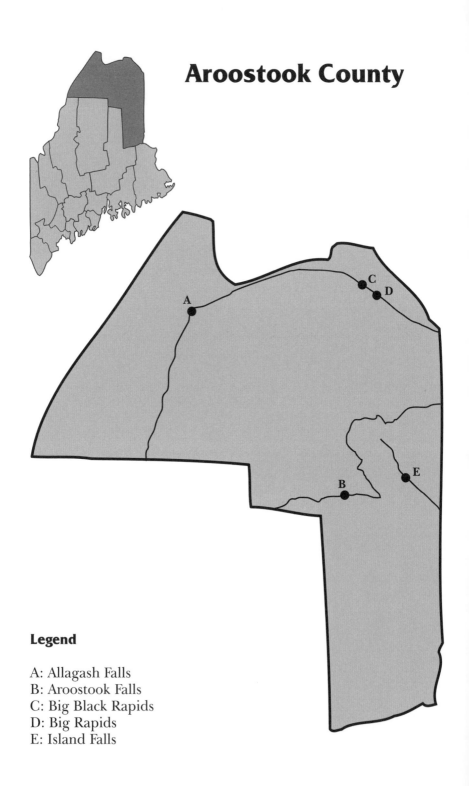

Aroostook County

Legend

A: Allagash Falls
B: Aroostook Falls
C: Big Black Rapids
D: Big Rapids
E: Island Falls

CHAPTER THREE

Aroostook County

Aroostook is a Micmac Native American word, meaning "beautiful" or "shining river." The St. John River, which flows through this county, rises and falls quickly, sometimes a foot or more in one day. This river can only be canoed in late spring.

When the British deported the French Acadians out of Canada, the British were unable to use their ships to follow them down the St. John River, due to the fast-moving river and impassable falls. In the logging era, the lumber industry wanted Allagash timber, but the St. John flowed south to north, which meant the timber could not easily travel to Bangor. So, they raised the water level in the lakes to reverse the flow of the river, and the logs were sent to market. Samuel de Champlain named this river when it was discovered on St. John the Baptist Day in 1604.

Many of the rare plants in Maine, New England, and the world, only grow in the St. John Valley in Aroostook County. Many of them grow next to the waterfalls in the area. The endangered plants that grow near waterfalls are as follows:

- Parnassia Glauca or Grass-of-Parnassus: solitary white flowers at the stem with green petals.
- Prenanthes Racemosa or White Glaucous Lettuce: a wildflower with a distinctive bluish-gray leave and a pinkish flower head.
- Triantha Glutinosa or Sticky False Asphodel: sticky stem thought to keep crawling insects from stealing the pollen or eating the flowers; flowers are mainly red.
- Anemone Multifida or Bird's-foot Anemone: a very rare plant; grows on calcareous gravel strands and ledge crevices near riverbanks.
- Primula Mistassinica or Bird's-eye Primrose (also known as Dwarf Canadian Primrose): grows on wet, calcareous ledge and rocks; flowers are pink, lilac, or white with a yellow eye.
- Purple Clematis Occidentalis: a rare and delicate lavender flowering plant.
- Castilleja Septentrionalis or Northern Painted Cup: a perennial herb with "hairy" stems and white purple-tinged flower.

- Hedysarum Alpinum or Alpine Sweet-broom: often grows on the upper portions of a river; has pea-like leaves and small, magenta, pea-like flowers.
- Pedicularis Furbhihiae or Furbish's Lousewort: a globally rare plant that requires a special habitat to grow; has a yellow flower and fern-like leaves and only grows on a narrow strip of a sloped riverbank, which is damp, not too close to the water, but close enough so the forest can provide shade.

A large portion of the St. John River Valley lies in Maine, but there is a fall area that is located at the mouth of the St. John River in Canada that is worth mentioning here. This reversing fall has an Abenaki legend of its origin. The split rock at the base is Glooscap's club, which he threw after smashing the dam that was there. Glooscap was one of the Abenaki great spirits. The original dam was called a Beavers Rolling Dam, which was actually first created by beavers. The tides here create a whirlpool and logs would often get caught whirling around for days. The Abenaki believed that this place was the dwelling of Manitou, who is the Abenaki Devil or evil spirit. This was a dangerous and strange place to the Native Americans, who once lived here.

Allagash Falls

Directions: I-95 to exit 286. Take ME 212 to ME 11 to ME 161 to Allagash. This site is not accessible by road.

This site is on the Allagash River, just before the Allagash River and the St. John River meet. The word *Allagash* is an Abenaki word that means "bark cabin" or "hemlock bark." The falls are located in Township 15, Range 11. These are slate falls with a thirty- to forty-foot total drop. Large boulders in the stream-bed cause the turbulent rapids. This is a series of drops, created by upturned, thin slate rocks, with many potholes on the bottom of the falls.

The Allagash River was thoroughly dynamited to ease the way for logging. In 1851, a dam was built over this difficult drop by a mutual beneficial corporation. What that meant was that the state provided the legal means where the logging companies collectively took charge of river improvements, protected their interests, and distributed costs among those who used the river commercially. At one time, these falls cost the lumber companies between $10,000 to $15,000 per year in losses.

There are many legends about this falls. One story is that a magical appearance of an old Native American man's face shows in the rock beneath the waterfalls. Why he appears is not known. There is also a legend of a ghost who appears on top of the falls. Supposedly, it is a ghost of a Native American maiden who threw herself off the ledge. She appears to the people who explore these falls and may get too close to the edge.

The area is also the spot of an old campsite, both Native American and logging. It is a portage site today, and only accessible by canoe.

The bedrock here is a near vertical bed of slate. It is part of the Seboomook Formation. The Seboomook Formation was created over 400 million years ago, when the ocean covered most of the northern part of Maine. There were massive young mountains here, and volcanoes were all over the area. Ocean currents deposited sand and mud, layer upon layer, from the materials that were eroded from the mountains. Lava erupted from fissures into the seawater to form oddly shaped deposits within the sand and mud in this area. The word *Seboomook* is Abenaki and means "small lake" or "at or near the large stream."

Waterfall Ratings

Aroostook Falls
(Also known as Aroostook Dam)

Directions: I-95 toward Canada. Take Provincial Route 2 to exit 104 (Aroostook Exit). Take Aroostook Road (unpaved) on left. There is a .2 distance from road to site.

This is the site of the most costly log jam in Maine's logging history. Aroostook Falls are on the Aroostook River in Township 7, Range 9. The spectacular log jam took place on May 8, 1880. It grew to epic proportions, spilling over the rim of the river and covering several acres. The logging companies had to wait until Fall when the jam finally broke, but there were too many logs when they reached these falls; in some places the logs were 200 feet thick. For four days, the logs kept coming, and actually started to go back *up* the falls! Finally in November, welcome rain occurred, and helped moved the logs down river smoothly.

Waterfall Ratings

Big Black Rapids

Directions: Go to Township 15 and ask for local directions.

Big Black Rapids is located on the St. John River in Township 15, Range 13. It contains rapids that are 4,100 feet in length. These are very unusual rapids; the river is wide here, and a large volume of water flows over an irregular riverbed creating complicated channels. The name comes from the fact that the water is brown to black from the tannic acid in it, and it is odorless. The water flow is extremely variable, depending on the time of year and rainfall.

This is in an extremely remote area, but has been used for thousands of years. Ancient writing has been found here. The area is on the National Registry of Historic Places.

The significant period for these rapids is between 4,000 BC to the twentieth century. Apparently, this place holds key evidence for deciphering the Native American use of the St. John River area. Also, it proves or shows contact between prehistoric inhabitants of the Bas Saint-Laurent (Quebec), the Lower St. John River area in New Brunswick, and the Allagash area in Maine.

Waterfall Ratings

Big Rapids

Directions: I-95 to exit 286. Take ME 212 to ME 11 to ME 161. Take left on Frank Mack Road.

Big Rapids are on the St. John River. They are located southwest of St. Clair Island in the Allagash. This is the widest and largest rapid site in the St. John Watershed. It is over 300 feet wide. The rapids occur where the river makes a sharp elbow turn and has developed over a lag deposit. They are located about seven miles above the confluence of the two rivers. It is rocky all over and was absolutely hated by the loggers who would run logs on the river. It is a forty-foot drop over two miles.

Big Rapids is also the habitat for a number of vascular plant species that are rare in Maine. The rare plants found here include: Furbish's Lousewort (Pedicularis Furbishiae); False Asphodel (Tofieldia Glutinosa—found only in St. John's River Valley); Glaucous White Lettuce (Prenanthes Racemosa); Grass of Parnassus (Parnassia Glauca), Northern Painted Cup (Castelleja Septentrionalis); Sweet Broom (Hedysarum Alpinus); Dwarf Canadian Primrose (Primula

Mistassinica). *The plants in this area are protected and the site should not be over-used or abused in any way.*

Waterfall Ratings

Island Falls

Directions: I-95 to exit 276. Take ME 159 to Bog Brook Road - take left to Island Falls.

The town of Island Falls is on the West Branch of the Mattawamkeag River. It was settled in the summer of 1843. Levi Sewall found an island and falls that he thought would be good for waterpower. The town is named for the falls on the island in the river. These were considered impassable falls and rapids at the time.

Clinochrysotile and Hedenbergite, dark green to black crystals, were found in this area. Hedenbergite is a rock-forming mineral, which is a "cousin" to the gemstone diopside. Good crystals of this mineral are very rare. Clinochrysotile is the monoclinic form of Chrysotile. The color varies from gray-white to golden yellow to green. It is a member of the serpentine group and has been mined as asbestos.

Waterfall Ratings

Directions: I-95 to exit 264. Take ME 11 to ME 158 to Moro Road (right turn). There is a .2 mile distance from road to destination.

This site is on East Hastings Brook in the Moro Plantation area. It is the largest of the five falls that lie on this brook. It is part of well-known falls in the area, which consists of Warren Falls, Stair Falls, Upper Falls, and Jackson Sluice. There is a twenty-six foot total drop that ranks among the top twenty falls in Maine. The lip of the falls is massive, a nearly flat ledge that crosses the entire stream. Water fans out as it drops, and is split in two by an outcropping of bedrock into a narrow left-hand column and a wider right-hand column. The pool at bottom of the falls shows signs that it may be used for swimming.

 Swimming in any rapid water can be dangerous and extreme caution should be exercised. Some of these areas are not patrolled that often, and help may be many miles away.

The bedrock is pelite and sandstone and there are lots of bugs in this remote spot.

Waterfall Ratings

Cumberland County

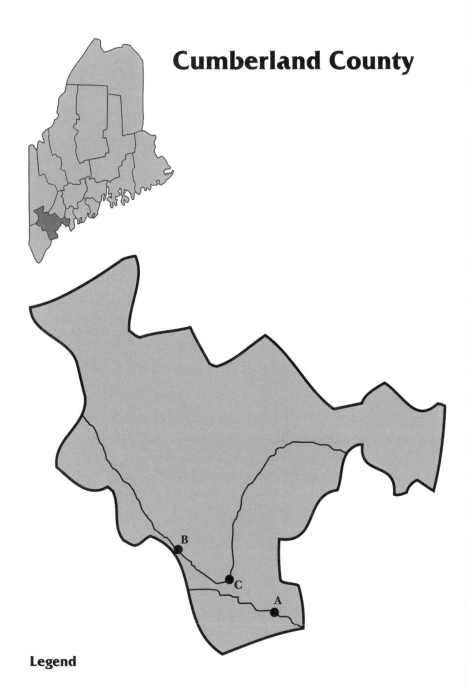

Legend

A: Bonny Eagle Falls
B: Dundee Falls
C: Mallison Falls

CHAPTER FOUR
Cumberland County

Bonny Eagle Falls

Directions: I-95 to exit 63 toward Windham. Take ME 202 to ME 115 to ME 35 to ME 25.

Located on the Saco River in the Hollis and Standish area, Bonny Eagle Falls is a natural falls described as a 48-foot drop over a horizontal run of 2,500 feet. The water divided into two channels at the head of the falls that formed an island of 60 acres.

There is a hydroelectric plant at this site today, drowning most of the falls. The dam also flooded a small area called "Indian Reservation." Until 1835, small bands of Native Americans would come there to fish.

The current name is said to come from folklore. Tradition states that a Scottish person was crossing a bridge here when he met another man. As an eagle flew over, he said, "Look at the bonny eagle," and the name stuck.

Waterfall Ratings

Capissic Falls

(Also known as—other Native American spellings—Capipissoke, Capissicke, Capessick, Capesseck, Capesseck, Capisseck, Kepiseke, Keppisich Falls)

Directions: I-95 to exit 103. Take ME 9 to US1A south to Cumberland Ave (take right).

These falls are located on Capissic Brook in Portland. The Native American word means "stopped up" or "the obstructed branch." The site was important to the Native Americans as the shortest route from the Fore River to the fishing station at Ammecongon on the Presumpscot River. Remember that the Abenaki would name sites as they came from the coast. As they canoed up to this fall site, it looked like a natural dam or a stopped-up river. Thus, the name of the falls. A dam downstream drowns these falls today. They were natural-ledge drops.

Waterfall Ratings

Dundee Falls
(Also known as Warren Falls; Dundee Pond Dam)

 Directions: I-95 to exit 63. Take 202 to ME 115 South to US 302, right on River Road to right on Down Home Road. There is a .3 mile difference between road and site.

These falls are on the Presumpscot River in the Gorham and Standish area and Presumpscot is an Abenaki word, meaning, "river of many falls," "many rough places," "broken rocks," or "ledges in the channel." There were many falls on this river, but they have been drowned today and no longer exist. The natural falls were cascade falls. This site was named for Dundee Bill Mason, who was an early settler.

One of the locks of the Cumberland and Oxford Canal, which operated from approximately 1830 to 1880, was located here. The Cumberland and Oxford Canal was the only canal built in Maine of any length. It was suppose to connect bodies of water with Portland Harbor. The canal opened on June 1, 1830, and was thirty-eight miles long. It flourished for twenty years, when the railroads started to take away their business.

Various minerals have been found here, which include Almandine or garnet, beryl, and andalusite. Andalusite is a polymorph with two other minerals (Kyanite and Sillimanite). A polymorph is a mineral that shares the same chemistry but a different crystal structure with another. The color is white, red, brown, orange, and green.

Spodumene was also found here. Spodumene is a rock-forming mineral. This is considered a new mineral; it was discovered only 300 years ago, and the gem variety was discovered only 120 years ago. The color comes in pink to lilac and is a unique find to gem collectors. Beryl has also been found here and is generally unknown to the public, but is a most-important gem mineral. The colorless (Goshenite) is a pure beryl, but impurities give it varied coloration. Emerald is green, Aquamarine is a blue color, greenish-yellow is Heliodor, pink is called Morganite, red is red beryl, and yellow is golden beryl. The color found in Maine is usually aquamarine.

The Kyanite found here were blue crystals and considered the best source of this mineral found in Maine. Kyanite is a polymorph with andalusite and sillimanite. The color is sapphire-like blue. It has a unique quality in that it varies in hardness in the same crystal (like a diamond). Ilmenite was also discovered here. This is an Iron Titanium Oxide and an economically-important mineral. It is the most vital ore of titanium. The color is usually iron black.

In 1954, large orange crystals of Microlite were discovered. This is a very bizarre find. Unfortunately, no known specimens exist today. Microlite generally contains impurities of radioactive elements called rare earths, so this mineral is somewhat radioactive. Microlite is the tantalum-rich member of the series of minerals and pyrochlore is the niobium rich member. The color can be pale yellow, reddish brown, red, olive, and emerald green.

Waterfall Ratings

Gambo Falls
(Also known as Gambo Falls Dam)

Directions: I-95 to exit 63. Take 202 to right on Newhall Road, which eventually becomes Gambo Road.

One of the mills at these falls was the Oriental Powder Company, a famous gunpowder plant. Many employees were killed at this dangerous mill in its heyday. The dam here now is on the Presumpscot River in the Gorham and Windham area. These are drowned falls today. There are still buildings from this mill at the site and the area is considered a Maine ghost town.

Waterfall Ratings

Mallison Falls
(Also known as Lock Falls; Horse Beef Falls; Naquamqueeg Falls; Mallison Falls Dam)

 Directions: I-95 to exit 48. Take ME 25 which becomes Cumberland Street, then becomes River Road. Turn left onto Mallison Falls Road.

Snow-white Scolecite was found here. It is the only known place in Maine where this mineral occurs. Scolecite is a rare mineral that forms in volcanic bubbles called vesicles. The color is clear to white. This site was located on the Presumpscot River. Presumpscot is a Native American word meaning, "many falls" or "many rough places." These are drowned falls today by a dam on site. The natural falls dropped eighteen feet. At one time, there was a woolen mill here, as well as two of the twenty-seven locks of the Cumberland and Oxford Canal. In 1763, the first bridge crossed the river at this place, which connected Gorham and Windham. Native Americans called these falls Naquamqueeg. They are the first set of falls above Saccarappa Falls.

The legend of these falls start in 1746, when a man named the "Scout," or Joe Wyer, found out that his sister, Anna, had been killed by the Native Americans here. Anna's daughter, Dorothy, so the story continues, was kidnapped by the tribe that killed Anna. They intended to sell her as a slave to the French in Canada. Joe immediately took off after his niece. Joe caught up with the kidnapers, sneaked behind the girl, and cut her ropes. As they started to escape, the Native Americans noticed what was happening. Joe killed the Native Americans; then Joe and Dorothy headed home.

What is most interesting about this legend is that there is also a Native American oral tale about this place. There was a farmer named Joe Weir. He came home one day and found that the Native Americans had burned his farm, killed any men who were there, and took the women into captivity. After that, he killed as many Native Americans as he could. Many years later, he was captured by the Native Americans and taken to a place above these falls. (It is thought that this placet may also be Lewiston Falls, but Horse Beef Falls are not too far away from Lewiston Falls.) Weir managed to untie himself and kill his guard. He built a fire on the high bank below the falls. The rest of the tribe paddled to that spot, and fell over the falls and died. What exactly happened there many have been erased by time, but it does show a clash of two cultures in the Maine wilderness in the 1700s.

As with most legends, there is usually a grain of truth to be found.

Waterfall Ratings

Steep Falls

(Also known as Dam Number One)

Directions: I-95 to exit 63. Take ME 202 to ME 115 to ME 35 to ME 25. Take right on Manchester Road, turn right on Royal Pine Drive to Steep Falls.

This is one positive and a success story of waterfall history in Maine. First, this stretch of river is not as polluted as the downstream part. This site is on the Presumpscot River in the Standish and Gorham areas. Second, this is a very scenic area and the falls are regulated. There is a twelve-foot drop, with four feet falling nearly vertically. A hydroelectric plant at the site operates off a canal that diverts water from the river more than a mile upstream. The water is returned at the side of the river immediately above the final pitch here, so the waterfall usually has adequate flow over the ledge. The plant is built well off the waterfall site and created a dam waterfall site here as well. This is considered the best example in the state of a hydroelectric plant being blended into a natural setting and not detracting from the site.

Waterfall Ratings

Yarmouth Falls

(Also known as Royal River Falls; Goochs Falls; Bakers Falls; Cotton Mill Falls; Sparhawk Dam; Pumgustuck—Native American name)

Directions: I-95 to exit 19. Take ME 109 to US1 and left on Shore Road.

This area is a park today. These falls are on the Royal River in the Yarmouth area. Yarmouth was named in honor of Yarmouth, England. The upper falls (Goochs Falls) has a dam on site. A fish ladder here allows the alewives to migrate through on their journey up the river. On the south side of the park, is an area called Shoe Shop Canal that was built in 1756. Downstream is Bakers Falls, which is a sloping ledge of a ten- to twelve-foot drop. Ruins of brick and stone mills are seen here. Further downstream is Sparhawk Dam, which is also called Cotton Mill Falls. There is a hydroelectric plant there today. The last fall site is called Pumgustuck Falls, which are rapids to the tidewater. The Native American name, Pumgustuck, means, "falls goes out place." The river ends with a fall site at the mouth. There is excellent fishing for brown trout at these falls.

Waterfall Ratings

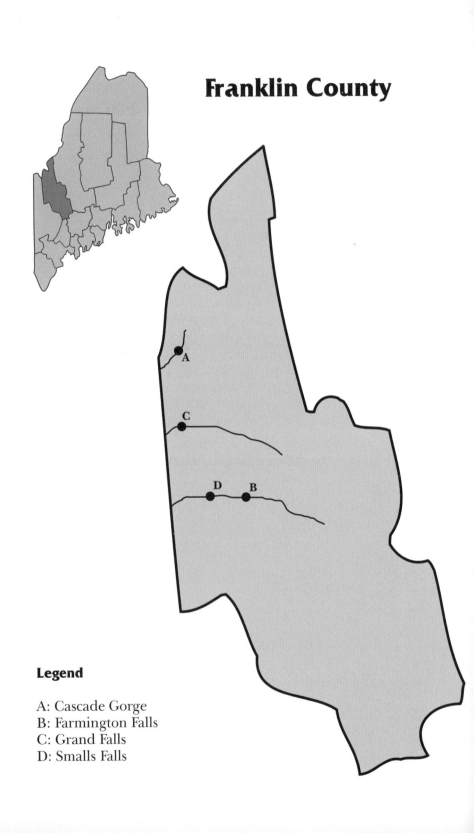

Franklin County

Legend

A: Cascade Gorge
B: Farmington Falls
C: Grand Falls
D: Smalls Falls

CHAPTER FIVE
Franklin County

The Sandy River has always been considered unnavigable because of the numerous rocks and low water. The Native American name was Mussel Unsquit, meaning "a place where Indians get plenty of moose," "a whole canoeful of game," or "a good hunting ground."

Alder Stream Falls

 Directions: Route 2 South. Take ME 201 to ME 148 to ME 8 to ME 16 to ME 27 to ME 142. Take right on Depot Street. There is a .2 mile difference from road to site.

These falls are on Alder Stream in Alder Stream Township, and are aptly named for the many alder trees that were once found here. Many gem-quality minerals and crystals have also been discovered, such as the Clinochrysotile, a light gray-green crystal. Hematite, which is a black hematite with bright red jasper has been discovered at this place as well. Hematite is an ore of iron. It is blood red color when in powder form and is used as a pigment. It gets its name from the Greek word, meaning "blood-like." Legend states that large deposits of hematite formed from battles that were fought and the blood that flowed into the ground. It is considered a rare mineral. The color can be gray, black, and red to brown.

Quartz and jasper have all been discovered here. Jasper is a variety of quartz. This variety is a dense and opaque, microcrystalline variety, usually red, brown, or yellow, and colored by oxides of iron, which gives it interesting patterns. It can actually be found in all colors. It is used as a decorative stone and is finely grained of Chalcedony. It was a favorite gem in ancient times. Folklore states that Jasper would drive away evil spirits and protect the wearer against snake and spider bites. It is also thought to bring rain and can align all the chakras and balance the yin-yang energies. It is stabilizing and healing.

Gold has been found in this stream as late as 1985. Gold is often discovered at the edges of whirlpools and in the tails of eddies, which is the bottom of a rapid. Ordinarily, gold does not travel far from its source and can only move when the water is running fast. That's one reason why gold may be found near waterfalls. For example, on the East Branch of Swift River near Coos Canyon, gold has been taken out of a series of waterfalls (one miner panned thirty-two ounces from here). Waterfall names were not always given to treasure/gold seekers. This is not surprising due to mining secrecy and not wanting someone to know where they were finding gold. However, it may also be true that the waterfalls may not have names or that the miners even knew the names.

Waterfall Ratings

Angel Falls

(Also known as Angel Wing Falls; Unknown Falls)

Directions: Route 2 South. Take ME 201 to ME 201A to ME 4 to ME 17. Turn left on Houghton Road, then right on Bemis Road. There is a .5 mile difference to site.

The location is in a deep canyon and is considered a hanging falls that formed in what geologists call a "hanging valley." A hanging valley is a valley that was formed when the glacier cut out the main valley floor after the side valley was cut. The falls are narrow at the top, widen in the middle, than narrow again at the bottom. This site is located on Mountain Brook in Township D-E, Range 6. This place was practically unknown until 1965, except by a few trappers, loggers, fishermen, and woodsmen. U.S. Geological Service Geologist, Dr. Robert H. Moench, rediscovered it that year. This site claims to be the largest drop in Maine, and at ninety feet, it is in a battle with Moxie Falls for that honor.

The falls were named because this waterfall looked like an angel's wing to some earlier visitor. These are horsetail waterfalls and are very unusual for Maine. The water is slightly brown in color with foam. This may come from the source of these falls, which is an upland swamp. There was a dam built across these falls in the logging era, but it collapsed in the 1920s.

There are two large drops with several cascades between each drop. There are two theories about how the single-drop waterfall was formed. The first theory is that erosion caused the drop. The second is that a perfectly-sized boulder at the base of the waterfall used to sit on the top and was knocked off by the Ice Age or a very powerful storm.

Gold and strautolite have been found here. Strautolite is usually silver to dark brown color and is a rock forming mineral of metamorphic origin. The bedrock is phyllite and is known as one of the largest exposures in the vicinity.

Waterfall Ratings

Cascade Gorge

Directions: Route 2 South. Take ME 201 to ME 27 to ME 4 to Sandy River Plantation.

This is an unusual place. The water is completely clear and odorless. These falls are on the Cascade Stream in Sandy River Plantation. This is a 2,200 foot V-shaped gorge with a depth of 100 feet. The total drop for these falls is 300 feet, but has several cascades in the range of two-foot to five-foot drops. The principal falls occur at the head of the gorge and have a nearly vertical drop of fifteen feet into a ledge-lined plunge pool. This is an important bedrock site of the Rangeley Formation, which consists of metaconglomerate interbedded with phyllite

41

containing altered staurolite. The gorge appears to have developed along the line of a fault. There are scoured potholes here that are several feet deep. This is a well-known tourist and scenic area today.

Waterfall Ratings

Farmington Falls
(Also known as Meesee Contee or Meesuncontu)

Directions: Route 2 South. Take ME 201 to ME 27 to ME 43, take left onto Broadway to Farmington.

This site is located on the Sandy River in village of Farmington. This place is actually partly in Farmington and partly in Chesterville. This is a series of small rapids and pitches. The area was named Farmington because it was considered a good farming area. The Native American village here was called Amascontee or Amaseconti, which means, "plenty of alewives." This was also the last known location of the Native American, Pierpole, before he left for an unknown destination, never to be seen again. He gave much of the early Native American information that we know today. He was the only Native American that remained when the first European settled here. He was made famous by a poem by Julia Ismay Harris.

There was a covered bridge here was built by Col. Thomas Lancaster in 1831. Some of this bridge was washed out in various floods during the 1850s. The concrete bridge was built in 1931.

Grossular Garnet was found at this site. Garnet is common in highly metamorphosed rocks or pegmatite rocks. It forms under high temperatures and pressure. Garnets are usually red, but have a wide range of colors. It is usually associated with topaz, beryl, tourmaline, vesuvianite, diopside minerals. Grossular Garnets come in a variety of colors. These types of garnets form in wollastonite, calcite, and vesuvianite. The colors are hessonite (red/brown); leuco (colorless); hydorgrossular (opaque

42

green); tsavolite/tsavorite (emerald green). The word, Grossular, comes from the Greek word, meaning gooseberry. It is the calcium aluminum garnet and the color orange is the most common.

Very large crystals of Vesuvianite have been found here. They were grayish brown crystals. Vesuvianite, also known as Idocrase, was originally found on Mount Vesuvius, hence the name, and is found in volcanic rock. The color is normally green, but can be brown, yellow, blue or purple. It is usually associated with garnets. White crystal Prehnite was also found in the Vesuvianite here. Prehnite is a mineral used as ornamental stone. It is usually green in color, so this was a rare find indeed.

Waterfall Ratings

Grand Falls

 Directions: Route 2 South. Take ME 201 to ME 148 to ME 16 to ME 27. Take right King and Bartlett Road, turn right onto Grand Falls Road.

A rare site in Maine is here. This is a beautiful and rare thirty-foot drop horseshoe waterfall. This site is on the Dead River in the Eustis area. The Dead River ironically gets its name from its dead calm waters, though this is a great fast water site. It is known as a nice spot to travel to by snowmobile. It is located eleven miles on a dirt road called the Kibby Camp Road.

Waterfall Ratings

Livermore Falls

 Directions: I- 95 to exit 109B. Take ME 133, then turn left on Church Street, right on Knapp Street and end at Livermore Falls.

These falls are on the Androscoggin River in Livermore. The natural falls were a twenty-two foot drop over five hundred feet, but the first fourteen-foot drop was vertical. A dam was built here in 1867 at the crest of the falls, adding seven feet to the total drop.

There was a covered bridge here that was built in 1872. This was a Haupt Truss bridge, which is rare in Maine. The bridge was destroyed in the flood of 1896.

The Native American name for this spot was Rokomeko, meaning "great corn land." The prehistoric village name was Namercante or Buccawganecants. The first European settlers came here in the 1770s and the village was called Port Royal. This site was named for Decon Elijah Livermore, after the first settler here.

Since the late 1800s, this area has been rich in railroad lore, papermaking, lumber and the logging industry.

There has been Rose Quartz and Beryl found here. Also, Staurolite and Vesuvianite were found in the early nineteenth century. This place in Maine produced the best gray and brown crystal Vesuvianite in the world.

Waterfall Ratings

Directions: Route 2 South. Take 201 and turn right on Heald Stream Road.

The rapids are really continuous steep pitches located on the Moose River in Township 2, Range 1. The river flows over ledge and boulders otherwise known as a lag deposit, which cause large standing waves to form during periods of high water. The bedrock is dark sandstone, shale, and quartzite. The trees on the north side of the river appear to be extremely an old growth. There is a natural population of landlocked salmon at this site.

It is also a fossil locality. Brachiopods have been found in the shale here. Brachiopod or "lamp shells" are marine fossils from the lower Cambrian era. This is the most abundant fossil found in Maine, though fossils of any kind are very rare in Maine. Brachiopods were shelled organisms that lived in both shallow and deep-water environments. Superficially, they resemble clamshells. These fossils can be found anywhere, because Maine has been completely under the ocean at least four different times. There are two major divisions of the Brachiopods; the articulates and the inarticulates. Only the hard brachiopod valves are commonly preserved as fossils.

Waterfall Ratings

Mosher Pond Stream Falls
(Also known as Rainbow Cascade)

Directions: Route 2 South. Take ME 201 to ME 27 to ME 43, take left onto Broadway to Farmington.

What is really fascinating about these falls is that from a geologic point of view, there is no compelling reason why they even exist. They may have been cut through dead ice during the ice age. Folklore stories tell that at the right time of day, the falls act as a prism on the sunlight that hits it, creating a spectacular rainbow. Perhaps it just exists for people to enjoy.

This area is located on an outlet stream from Mosher Pond which is a tributary to Barker Stream in Farmington. The site is named for John Mosher, a settler here in 1855. The main falls are a vertical drop of thirty-five feet into a gorge. There is an upper section with several drops, totaling seventeen feet. The lower section is several small drops often to fifteen feet. The water is colorless with no odor. The bedrock is quartzite and slate, which tend to weather to a brown color.

Waterfall Ratings

Directions: Route 2 South. Take ME 201 to ME 4. Take left onto Phillips Road, end at Smalls Falls Rest Area.

This is a slate waterfall and a mineral heaven. These falls are found on the Sandy River in Township E. This waterfall site is located twelve miles south of Rangeley, and is possibly named for the Small family, who owned much of the land in the area at one time.

These mountain waterfalls occur at a junction of two streams. The falls drop a total of sixty feet. The first set of falls is a vertical cascade. The second set is a vertical fan horsetail. The third set is a vertical plunge and segmented horsetail. The fourth set is a horsetail and slide. The falls lie on top of Perry Mountain and flows over black, rusty shale. The black color is due to the graphite or sulfur and the rust is due to iron sulfide minerals in the ground. The water color is slightly brown, probably because of the land that the falls flow over. The falls have developed over a strike and formed on faults and folds. The bedrock is volcanic metamophosized rock. The previous owners donated this site to the state.

Chalcopyrite, andalusite, and phlogopite or black mica, has been found here. There are "Maltese Crosses" of chiastolite found here, which is a variety of andalusite. Phlogopite is a rare member of mica group and not well known. It is mined for heat and electrical insulating properties and considered the best mineral in the mica family. The color is light to dark brown. Mica is an important group of sheet minerals. It is a rock-forming mineral and is found in all three types of rocks igneous, metamorphic, and sedimentary. This mineral is flexible and brittle, and can withstand high temperatures and pressure. Reddish-brown biotite is the most common mica found in the rocks. This mineral was also very important building material to the Inca people of Peru. They used this mineral, as well as quartz, to build their temples. They believed that it was an enchanted mineral and helped to increase spiritual energy. Chalcopyrite is a copper pyrite. It is a bright golden color, and has often been confused with pyrite and gold. It is a common mineral, and will tarnish to blue, green, yellow, and purple. The occurrence of this mineral is sporadic in Maine.

Clinochlore, cordierite, and Dravite have also been found here. Dravite is a little known species of the Tourmaline group. Its color is light brown to dark brown. It can be found in massive amounts here. Cordierite is not a well-known mineral. Its gemstone is called iolite. It has an unusual blue-violet color and is sometimes called a "water sapphire." It also has a color changing property called pleochroism.

Rutile, Jarosite, Margarite, and Pyrrhotite has also been found here. Rutile is a major ore of titanium. It also has major importance to the gemstone markets. Microscopic inclusions of rutile in quartz, tourmaline, ruby, sapphire, and other gemstones produces light effects such as "cat' s eye" and asterisms or stars. The color is black to reddish brown and found in large thick crystals or golden yellow to rusty yellow as inclusions or in thin crystals. Margarite is a white-gray mineral. The name comes from the Greek word, Margaritos, meaning pearl. It is part of the mica group. Jarosite is not a common mineral. The color is amber yellow to brown. Pyrrhotite, when found here is usually rust encrusted and produces an obnoxious sulfurous odor when broken, is an iron sulfide and has some unusual properties. First, it has an unusual formula. The amount of sulfur varies by roughly twenty percent to the amount of iron. Second, it has two symmetries. In natural pyrrhotite crystals, both phases are present in the same crystal. Third, it is magnetic, though weakly. It is the second most common magnetic mineral next to magnetite. Good crystals are rare to find. The color is bronze. This site is part of the Katahdin Deposit, which is the largest metallic mineral deposit in Maine.

Waterfall Ratings

Directions: Route 2 South. Take ME 201 to ME 148 To ME 8 to ME 16 to ME 27. Take next two left turns to South Road. Go right to Alder Stream Road.

The name probably comes from folklore. It was said that this ridge was so steep, that a climber had to hold on by their toenails. It is a series of five falls, located on Alder Stream in Alder Stream Township. The upper falls form the head of an enormous gorge in which all the other falls occur. The first set is a twenty-foot vertical fall over a massive ledge. It actually separates into two columns that are separated by an outcropping of ledge. The second set is a twenty-foot fan shaped falls. The water on top is churned silky white when it is forced through a narrow channel. On the north side, there is an extremely massive ledge. One section of that ledge is completely dry, but worn smooth, suggesting that the stream was once split here into a pair of falls. The third drop is five feet. Many minor hydraulic features are here. The fourth set of falls drops three feet, then drops another seven feet into a plunge pool. The cliffs around this pool are thirty-three to fifty feet high. The fifth set of falls occurs as the stream is leaving the gorge. The first drop is two feet through a narrow chute, then drops ten feet, then drops seven feet. The bedrock is quartzwacke and pelite and it is on a fault line. This is a favorite fishing spot for brook trout.

Waterfall Ratings

Hancock County

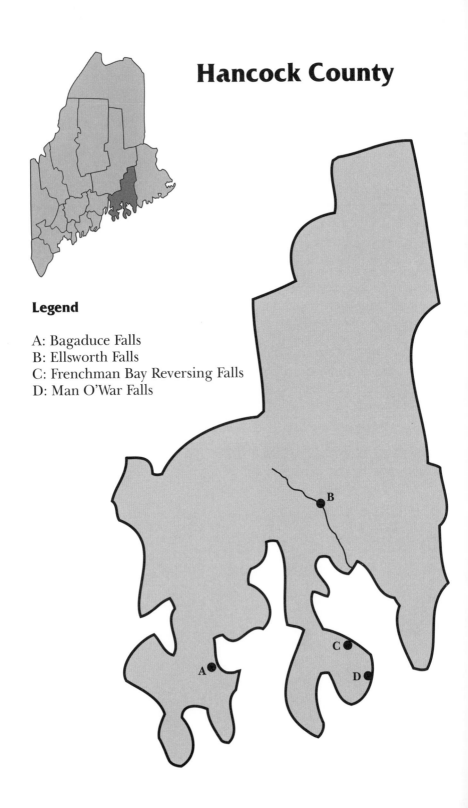

Legend

A: Bagaduce Falls
B: Ellsworth Falls
C: Frenchman Bay Reversing Falls
D: Man O'War Falls

CHAPTER SIX
Hancock County

Directions: I-95 to exits 182A. Take US1 exit 6A to ME 3 to ME 102. Take left to Beech Hill Road.

These falls are on Mount Desert Island in Acadia National Park and are a tourist site today.

Waterfall Ratings

Bagaduce Falls

Directions: I-95 to exit 174. Take ME 69 to US 1A to ME 174 to ME 3 N to ME 175 to ME 176. There is a .2 difference from road to site.

Here are tide or reversing falls that occur between Snow Cove and the Bagaduce estuary. These are salt-water falls in Brooksville area. There are actually three sets of falls northeast to the Narrows. At high tide, it was possible to navigate a large ship here, but otherwise these are basically impassable falls. Bagaduce is a Micmac word that means "big tideway river." The entire region was called Majabaga-duce. Today, it is used as a practice site for kayakers and canoeists.

Any falls that are near the coast are reversing falls, which are really tidal phenomenon, not actual technically falls. Rocks are situated in a narrow passage of tidal water where the volume and height of current reach the passage is significant. When the tidal current strikes the rocks, it tumbles over them, and to a lower level of land. Then, the tide reverses, and eventually the difference in water level again becomes significant forming the falls in the opposite direction.

Waterfall Ratings

Blue Hill Falls

(Also known as Fire Falls; Blue Hill Tide Falls;Awanadjo, Kallejedjwok, Kuladamitchwan)

Directions: I-95 to exit 174. Take ME 69 to US 1A to ME 174 to ME 3 N to ME 175 to ME 176.

This set of falls is the best reversing falls in Maine. The name Blue Hill comes because the area looked blue to settlers from a distance due to the spruce and pine trees that were once there. These reversing falls are three miles from the center of Blue Hill on the eastern end of the salt strait called Benjamin River. The falls are salty when the tide rises, and less salty when the tide ebbs. Native Americans called the hill that watches over the harbor, Awanadjo, meaning "small misty mountain." The site is really two rapids, one on the incoming tide and one on the outgoing tide. The falls are about six hundred feet long. High standing waves, and a reverse eddy also occur during the in-coming tide.

Molybdenite and Scheelite have been found. Scheelite is rarely found crystallized, but gray crystals were discovered here. Scheelite is an important ore of tungsten. It is named for the discoverer of tungsten, K.W. Scheele. This site is where supply of tungsten comes from for the United States. The color is white, yellow, orange, or greenish-gray to brown. This mineral also fluoresces blue under short wave ultraviolet light.

Wolframinte and Ferberite have also been discovered. Wolframite is actually a series between two minerals; Huebnerite and Ferberite. Huebnerite is the manganese rich part and ferberite is the iron rich part of the mineral. The color is black to gray to brown. This mineral is a mix of the two. If there is eighty percent manganese, it will be called Huebnerite or if eighty percent iron, it will be called Ferberite. Everything in between is called Wolframite. Ferberite is black in color, and much more rare to find than Huebnerite and Wolframite.

Waterfall Ratings

Ellsworth Falls

(Also known as Ledgefalls Dam; Ellsworth Dam; Ellsworth Power House and Dam)

 Directions: I-95 to exit 182A. Take ME 15 South to ME 9 to ME 179 to destination.

Originally, there were seven falls that existed in the two-mile stretch between Ellsworth and Ellsworth Falls. This particular fall area is on the Union River. The river drops eighty-five feet in just two miles. There is a dam here today, called Ledge Falls dam. The falls are made with black mica and named for Oliver Ellsworth, who was a delegate from Massachusetts to the Constitutional Convention in the 1700s. In 1985, this water phenomena was added to the National Registry of Historic Places due to the logging history of the area. It is also where prehistoric Native Americans lived. The village was called Precante, and it may have been inhabited during the Early Archaic period or Early Horticultural period.

Waterfall Ratings

Frenchman Bay Reversing Tidal Falls

Directions: I-95 to exit 182A. Take US 1 to East Side Road, turn left onto Tidal Falls Road (unpaved) and end at site.

These are reversing tidal falls located just off Route #1 in Hancock on the Taunton River. There is a Preserve and short hikes all through this area.

Waterfall Ratings

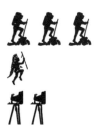

Goose Falls

(Also known as Goose Pond Dam)

Directions: I-95 to exit 174. Take ME 69 to US 1A to ME 174 to ME 3 to ME 175 to ME 176 to right on Cape Rosier Road to right on Goose Falls Road.

The place was named for the many geese once found in the area. These are reversing falls at the outlet of Goose Pond in the Brooksville area. The Native Americans called this carry or portage site, Edalichichiquassik, which means "where there is a very narrow place." Today, canoes and kayaks use it for practice and a great run. There is a dam here today.

Aurichalcite has been found. This mineral forms in the oxidation zones of zinc-copper deposits. The color is grass to pale green. It can be a bluish color, as well. There is also a copper mine at the falls. Copper has been mined here for centuries and is now depleted as an economically viable ore. The color of the mineral is brown or copper, and it does tarnish green.

Waterfall Ratings

Hadlock Brook Falls

(Also known as Waterfall Bridge Waterfall)

Directions: I-95 to exit 182A. Take US 1A to ME 3 to ME 198. There is a .7 mile walk from road to site.

It is a forty-foot waterfall that flows under a bridge on Mount Desert Island in Acadia National Park on a carriage road.

Waterfall Ratings

This footbridge is a forty-foot waterfall that flows under a bridge on Mount Desert Island in Acadia National Park on a carriage road.

Man O' War Falls

Directions: I-95 to exit 182A. Take US 1A to ME 3 to ME 102 to Main Street.

This waterfall plunges directly into the sound in Acadia National Park on Mount Desert Island from Man O' War Brook. It is a ten-foot vertical drop. The falls cascade down a granite face to a stone beach on Somes Sound, which is the large salt water Fjord that protrudes into Mount Desert Island.

The origin of the name is fascinating. Back in the era when warships and privateers roamed the North Atlantic, they usually were out of fresh drinking water when they reached this place. So, the ships would sail into the salt water of Somes Sound, and stop to refill their water from the Man O' War Falls, which was not brackish, because the swift motion of the falls kept any salt from mixing with the stream. Shells also surround the bottom of the falls. The best time to view falls is in the spring at low tide. There are no other falls that drop directly into the Atlantic Ocean in the state.

Waterfall Ratings

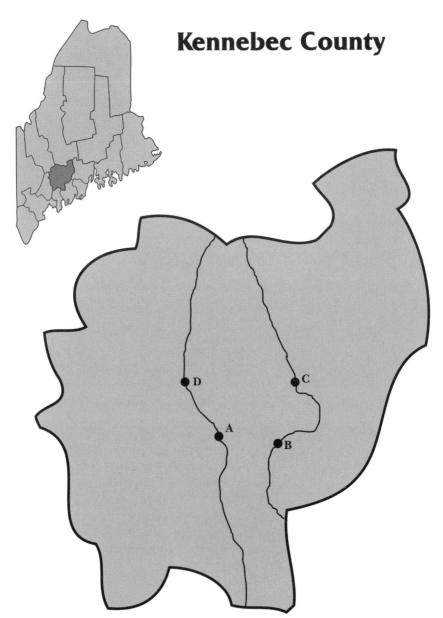

Kennebec County

Legend

A: Ancient Falls at Cushnoc
B: Benton Falls
C: Burnham Falls
D: Teconnet Falls

CHAPTER SEVEN
Kennebec County

The Kennebec and Dead Rivers meet the area called The Forks. Even in 1761, these rivers were considered difficult, rapid, and dangerous, and going upriver was the most difficult part when traversing on them.

The Kennebec River is the main river that Benedict Arnold traveled on his trek to Canada. It is said that he knew how difficult it was to travel upriver during low water, and yet he still tried to beat the river. He had many difficulties and lost many men during the trek through Maine.

The word Kennebec or quen-ne-bec is an Abenaki word, meaning "long blade." The name could also be the name of a chief named "Cannibis," who once lived on banks of the river. There is a third legend for the name Kennebec. It is the name of a rattlesnake god, who was sacred to Native Americans, called Monitou Kinnibec. The river was named because it was shaped like the snake.

After 157 years of pollution and destruction, this is the only river in New England that still has limited reproducing populations of all seven species of native fish found in Maine. Between 1780 and 1890, commercial fishing for Atlantic Salmon was extensive along here. In 1873, 15,000 salmon were taken from the river. That number dwindled to only forty salmon in 1947, which was the last year of legal commercial salmon fishing on the Kennebec.

The last log drive was in 1976 along the Kennebec River. The recreational use of the river really started after that year. Before then, the paper companies owned the river, and it was too crowded with logs to be used for anything other than log drives for many years.

Ancient Falls at Cushnoc
(Also known as Augusta Falls; Edwards Dam)

Directions: I-95 to exit 113. Take ME 3 to ME 104. Take sharp left onto Washington Street to right onto Waldo Street.

This was a favorite Native American spot; it was used as camping, hunting, and fishing grounds located on the Kennebec River in Augusta. This water phenomena also has appeared and disappeared at various times in its history. The dam is gone today. In the 1990s, twelve dams were breeched in Maine, including this dam. Now, the fish can migrate through this area, as they did in previous centuries.

It is a fifteen-foot drop, and considered one of several prehistoric trading routes to western Maine and Canada. The Abenaki word, Cushnoc, means "point one met the current" or "where the current overruns the tide." There is also a legend here that says that the name of this ancient trading post really is an old Norse word, Koussinock, meaning "place above the tide." It is thought that perhaps even the Norse sailors made it to this area.

This spot was a subsistence fishery for Native Americans between 1100 B.C. and 1500 A.D. Originally, Atlantic Salmon came up to this spot, 144 miles from the sea, and even further upriver to the Waterville area. In the 1800s, fishermen took 4,000 salmon from these falls alone. The dam was removed in 1999, one of the twelve dams that were removed in the 1990s that finally allowed the falls and the fish to return. On this spot, the stone and timber crib dam could still be seen on the banks of the river, first built in 1837, to support the textile mills located here.

Waterfall Ratings

Directions: I-95 to exit 138. Take left to Hinckley Road, which becomes Baker Street. Take right to ME 11 that becomes Clinton Avenue.

At one time, there were upper and lower falls located on the Sebasticook River in Benton. The lower falls are really considered rapids, and today the dam at this site has drowned the upper falls.

This is a good fishing spot for small mouth bass, pickerel, and white perch. American Eels use this spot for migration to the sea to spawn. As recent as 2001, this is another place where there has been controversy because the turbines in the dam kill the American Eels as they make their way to the ocean.

This area was named for Thomas Hart Benton, who was a democrat and congressman from Missouri. In 1989, this site was added to the National Registry of Historic Places. The period of significance is 1000 B.C. to 1000 A.D. The Native American tribes also used this area for fishing during this era.

I was allowed to go to the top of this dam for photos and an unique perspective of the river.

Waterfall Ratings

Burnham Dam

 Directions: I-95 to exit 157. Take ME 100 to Johnson Flat Road.

This spot is located on the Sebasticook River in Burnham. The word Sebasticook is Abenaki, meaning "almost through place."

Waterfall Ratings

Clinton Falls
(Also known as Fifteen-Mile Rips)

 Directions: I-95 to exit 138. Take left to Hinckley Road, which becomes Baker Street. Take right to ME 11. Turn left onto Railroad Avenue.

It is better classified as rapids, located on the Sebasticook River in the Clinton area.

Waterfall Ratings

Cobbosseecontee Lake Dam

 Directions: I-95 to exit 109B. Turn left onto Pond Road. Turn left onto Red Paint Road, stay straight onto Rylan Road.

Small mouth bass was first introduced into Cobbosseecontee Lake in Manchester in 1869. In 1976, this historic place was added to the National Registry of Historic Places. The period of significance is from 3000 to 1999 B.C. There is evidence here that this was a spot for seasonal use for fishing by prehistoric residents. The Native Americans would fish for salmon, alewife, sturgeon, or eels here. Cobbosseecontee Stream is in the Gardiner area. There are eight falls here with a total drop of 127 feet. The name is Abenaki, meaning, "plenty of sturgeon."

Waterfall Ratings

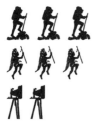

Teconnet Falls

(Also known as Ticonic Falls; Tacconnet Falls; Taconic Falls; Lockwood Dam; Katakouan, which is the Native American name)

 Directions: I-95 to exit 130. Take ME 104 to ME 201, turn left onto Benton Avenue.

These incredible falls are located on the Kennebec River in the Waterville area. This was an awesome fishing area in earlier times. In the spring of 1824, 5,200 pounds of alewives were taken from these falls. In early 1800s, fishermen took 4,800 salmon from here. No one is really sure what the Native American words mean. They could mean "the biggest," as in the biggest place to cross the Kennebec River, or they could just mean "a place to cross." It was a thirteen-foot drop, when the first mill was erected in 1784. There was a covered railroad bridge here in the early 1850s. The 1869 flood destroyed this Kennebec and Portland railroad bridge.

Benedict Arnold had to deal with this waterfall in 1775 as he was marching to Quebec City. The troops had to take their boat, called a "bateau," apart and carry the pieces around the falls. The boat never fit together correctly after this, which is not surprising because they used green wood, instead of seasoned wood to build the boat. They were instructed by the Native Americans how to build the correct canoe that would work in these fast, turbulent waters, but they decided to build a larger type of boat. It could carry more weight with less boat.

During the wet season, a large waterfall appears, and during the dry season, you can actually walk across this area. The falls were developed over a continuous ledge of hard slate that crosses the Kennebec River diagonally. There is a manufacturing plant and dam at the site today.

Waterfall Ratings

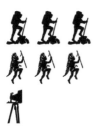

Wayne Village Dam

Directions: I-95 to exit 109B. Take ME 202 to ME 133 W, turn left onto Memorial Park Lane.

This dam site is located on the Kennebec River in Wayne and is found in an area of ancient sand dunes. Paleo-Native American artifacts have been discovered here. Evidence found suggests that some of the artifacts came from New York, Vermont, Pennsylvania, Nova Scotia, and from northern Maine. It seems to prove that trade and transportation was obviously accomplished in these ancient times.

Waterfall Ratings

Knox County

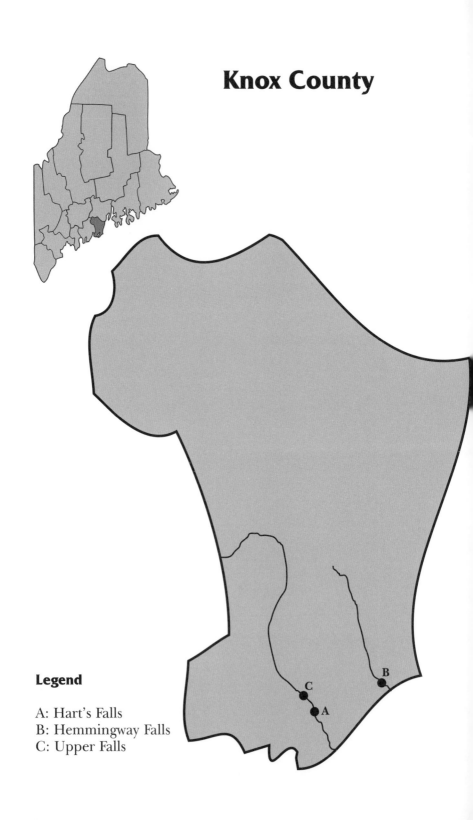

Legend

A: Hart's Falls
B: Hemmingway Falls
C: Upper Falls

CHAPTER EIGHT

Knox County

Ammacongan Falls
(Also known as First Falls)

 Directions: I-95 to exit 161. Take ME 7 to ME 131 to ME 90 to US 1 to ME 97. Turn left on Salt Pond Road, take right onto Pleasant Point Road and left on Harbor Lane.

A favorite Native American fishing spot on the St. George River. When the European settlers first arrived in this area, the Native Americans marked a tree near these falls and forbade the settlers to fish above it. This caused another major conflict between the Native Americans and Europeans. There were stories by then that when the settlers arrived, and started to build dams, the fish soon stopped coming. It was a matter of survival for the Native Americans. This was just the beginning of trouble over Native American fishing spots. Things were going to get worse, especially in York County, and will be discussed at future waterfall sites.

Waterfall Ratings

Hart's Falls

 Directions: I-95 to exit 161. Take ME 7 to ME 131. Take Main Street to Riverside Street in Warren.

Archaeological evidence suggests that this area may have been one of most important areas to the Natives. Cemetery sites were found here in the 1920s. This may have been the site called Wowinak, meaning "loop in River." This was a Penobscot tribe semi-permanent village in the era of 900 years B.P. or in the late ceramic period. These falls are found on the St. George River in Warren, and named for John Hart, who was a settler in the 1700s.

Waterfall Ratings

Hemmingway Falls
(Also known as Knox Mills Falls; Megunticook Falls)

  Directions: I-95 to exit 161. Take ME 9 to ME 7 to US 1 to Camden.

They are cascade waterfalls. The name is Malecite or Micmac meaning "big mountain harbor," or "rough waves." The falls are only 4,000 feet from the tidewater with a total drop of ten feet on the Megunticook River in Camden. There is also a dam on the site, but the waterfalls do still exist.

Waterfall Ratings

Lermond Mill
(Also known as Morgan's Mill)

  Directions: I-95 to exit 161. Take ME 7 to ME 131 to ME 235, then a right onto Common Road.

Today, the site is known as Morgan's Mill and it makes water-only mix in the bag recipes for campers, boaters, hikers, and fishermen. This is a restored nineteenth-century gristmill that grinds whole grain flours by waterpower. This site is located on Lermond Pond in Union Village. In 1984, the place was added to the National Registry of Historic Places. The period of significance is 1800 to 1849.

Waterfall Ratings

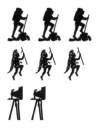

Upper Falls

(Also known as Warren Falls; Warren Sawmill Pond Dam; Knox Falls)

 Directions: : I-95 to exit 161. Take ME 7 to ME 131. Take Main Street into Warren.

This place is the centerpiece of park in Warren on the St. George River. Today, the pitch of five feet is a portage site for canoes. Ruins of mills can still be seen. It is a breeding ground for American Eels. The bedrock is sulfuric, carbonaceous pelite.

In 1793, a plan was developed for building a canal from the Sennebec Pond to the mouth of the St. George River in Warren. There would be three locks, including one here. The plan was un-feasible and abandoned in 1794. In 1970, this site was added to the National Registry of Historic Places. The period of significance was 1825 to 1849.

Waterfall Ratings

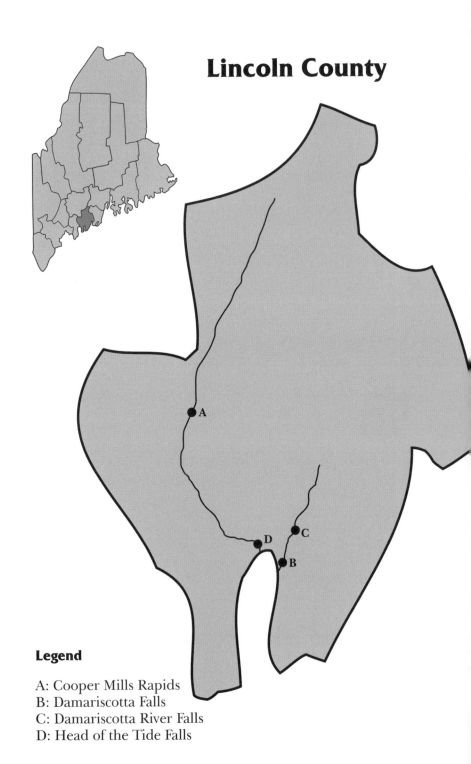

Lincoln County

Legend

A: Cooper Mills Rapids
B: Damariscotta Falls
C: Damariscotta River Falls
D: Head of the Tide Falls

CHAPTER NINE
Lincoln County

Coopers Mills Rapids
(Also known as Sheepscot River Whitewater Rapids; Above Head Tide)

 Directions: I- 95 to exit 113. Take ME 3 to ME 17. Take left onto Main Street, left onto Windsor Road.

These rapids are on the Sheepscot River in Whitefield. This place was named for Leonard Cooper, who was a settler here in 1833. There was gold mining done at this site at one time. It is also an important Atlantic Salmon spawning ground.

In March 2006, it was reported that the dam leaks and that the Atlantic Salmon can not always use the fish ladder because of lack of water. There is a controversy in town that some people want the dam taken down to allow the fish safe passage, while others say that the pond that the dam creates is the only water to use if, and when, a fire breaks out in the downtown area. The issue is still being discussed to find a positive solution as of this writing.

Waterfall Ratings

Damariscotta Falls

(Also known as Damariscotta Mills; Damariscotta Freshwater Falls; Damariscotta Lake Dam)

 Directions: I -95 to exit 103. Take ME 126 to ME 27 to ME 96. Take left onto King Philips Trail, turn left onto Boothbay SHRS. There is a .7 difference from road to site.

The Passamaquoddy word for these falls was Pedaukgowack meaning "place of thunder." The first Europeans reported that the falls at the headwater of Damariscotta River were extremely loud. Damariscotta is an Abenaki word, meaning "plenty of alewives." These falls are found on the Damariscotta River in Newcastle. The upper falls, which are fresh water, drop fifty feet into a salt-water reservoir below or the lower falls. This is a continuous series of cascades over bedrock. The water color is slightly green with an odor, and there is foam in the eddies.

Waterfall Ratings

Damariscotta River Falls

(Also known as Salt-water Falls; Damariscotta Tidewater Falls)

 Directions: I -95 to exit 103. Take ME 126 to ME 27 to ME 96. Take left onto King Philips Trail, turn left onto Boothbay SHRS.

These are reversing falls in Newcastle located on the Damariscotta River. The river is really an inlet of the ocean. These falls are brackish and below the fresh water falls above. In the 1700s, Father Rasle, in Jesuit Relations, wrote that during the fish months, one could fill 50,000 barrels a day. The fish were crowded together one foot deep.

Today, canoeists use the falls as a practice run. It is also a good fishing spot for stripers and mackerel.

Waterfall Ratings

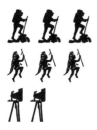

Head of the Tide Falls

(Also known as Head Tide Dam)

 Directions: I-95 to exit 103. Take I-295 to exit 51. Take 201 to ME 27 to ME 194. Turn left onto Head Tide Road.

Upstream from the dam in the freshwater, non-tidal part of the river, a globally uncommon brook floater mussel, Alamidonta Varicosa, is found. Brook Floaters are currently listed as a special concern in Maine. It is very uncommon and rarely found in abundance anywhere in the state.

It is located six miles upstream from Sheepscot Reversing Falls on the Sheepscot River in Alna and is better classified as rapids. The natural drop was ten to thirteen feet, but there is a dam here now. It is a fishing spot for Atlantic Salmon. This dam was built in 1762 and there was a covered bridge here in 1944. The bridge was built as a box pony truss bridge.

Waterfall Ratings

Oxford County

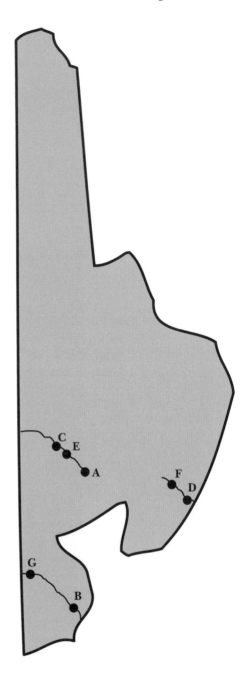

Legend

A: Devils Horseshoe
B: Hiram Falls
C: Mother Walker Falls
D: Rumford Falls
E: Screw Auger Falls
F: Snow Falls
G: Swans Falls

CHAPTER TEN

Oxford County

Aziscohos Falls

(Also known as Aziscohos Falls Whitewater Rapids; Aziscohos Lake Falls; Magalloway Dam; Aziscohos Dam)

 Directions: Route 2 South. Take ME 201 to ME 16 to ME 27 to ME 142 to ME 149 to ME 4 to ME 16 (again). Turn right onto Dam Road, then turn right.

There are exceptionally steep pitches and hydraulics found here. These rapids are located on the Magalloway River in Lincoln Plantation. This geologic area is a good example of rapids forming over a lag deposit. The first mile of this rapid, 1.8 miles in length, is considered impassable. There are three- to five-foot standing waves, large eddies, and cross currents in a boulder-strewn channel. Some of the boulders are thirteen feet in diameter. This mile is the steepest gradient documented to date on a large Maine river. The word Aziscohos is Native American for "small pine trees." White pine, one of the largest and abundant pine trees in New England at one time, is the Maine state tree.

One of Maine' s most famous Native Americans, Chief Metallak, known as the "Lone Indian of the Magalloway," lived here for twelve years. Several geographic sites are named for him and the Parmachenee Lake along the upper Magalloway is named after his daughter who tended to him when he was blinded in his later years. Magalloway is an Abenaki word, meaning "the shoveler," which was the name that the Native Americans gave to the Caribou.

As an interesting side note, during the Depression era, the men who were building the dam here actually made more money by panning for gold, than they did building the dam, so there is gold to be found, if the seeker knows where to hunt.

Waterfall Ratings

Basin Falls
(Also known as Basin Falls Brook)

Directions: I-95 to exit 109B. Take ME 133W to ME 219 to ME 117.

A strange unknown mineral in Maine is claimed to be found here: Alum, though this is highly suspect claim, because of such a wet climate around a waterfall and alum is a water-soluble mineral. It could, however, be a post mine growth. There are many abandoned mines in the area. The claim, according to C.T. Jackson in 1838 from the Second Report on the geology of the state of Maine says:

> "The gneiss is charged with pyrites due to the spray of falls – surface is kept moist and rapid decomposition takes place. Eventually through this process, sulfuric acid is formed and eventually creates potash or common alum."

Alum is a salt used in papermaking and in the tanning of skins. True (potash) alum is chemically a double salt of aluminum. It is water soluble, and is acidic when dissolved in water. Though it is mentioned as a mineral near a waterfall, the fact that it is water-soluble makes it highly suspect and is probably a typo or misidentification.

These falls are on Basin Falls Brook in Buckfield and are three segmented or tiered falls. The first set of falls is a broken twenty-six foot cascade that enters a large plunge pool. The second set is a ten-foot sloping cascade over a rough ledge. The brook then precedes about fourteen feet before dividing into left and right branches as the third set of falls appears. It is a pair of fifteen-foot broken falls separated by an intervening rock face twenty feet in height. These twin falls pour into opposite ends of a large plunge pool that is approximately twenty-three feet long and forty-six feet wide. The bedrock is limestone and dolostone. This site can be found hiking on the Royce Trail.

Waterfall Ratings

Cobb Brook Falls
(Also known as Cabb Brook Falls)

Directions: I-95 to exit 109B. Take ME 133W to ME 219 to ME 117 to ME 124. Turn right onto Hebron Station Road, turn right onto Sodom Road.

Niagara Falls are in New York and Canada, however the falls that occur here were also created due to the water undercutting the rock, just like Niagara Falls. These are the only falls like this in Maine. It is a single ten-foot drop, and the water color is clear with no odors. Located on Cobb Brook in the Hebron area, the place was named for William Cobb, a Revolutionary War Veteran and an early settler to the region.

The bedrock is quartz-muscovite phyllite, which weathers to a brown color. The falls appear to have developed by selective erosion of a basalt dike, which passes over the lip of the falls. There is probably a fault in this area.

Waterfall Ratings

Coos Canyon Falls

Directions: Route 2 South. Take ME 201 to ME 201A to US 2W to ME 17.

The gold found here was used in making the Maine State necklace. An old trail once connected this site with Augusta, Maine, and Coos, New Hampshire, which is probably the origin of the name of the canyon. The Native American word coos, means "crooked," and usually referred to a river.

These falls are located on the Swift River in Byron. There is a five-hundred-foot gorge created by the Swift River, and several falls are within the gorge, with a total drop of about twenty-five feet. The single largest drop is four feet. The water is slightly brown, but has no odor. The bedrock is phyllite with interbedded quartzite, and has exceptional examples of staurolite crystals. There are numerous outstanding erosion features here.

Waterfall Ratings

Devils Horseshoe

Directions: Route 2 South. Take ME 201 to ME 201A to US 2W to ME 108 to ME 26. Turn right onto Bear River Road.

There are numerous places in New England named Devil. Remember this is a Puritan colony and the Devil was seen everywhere in this vast wilderness. It was a truly frightening place in earlier times, and the rivers and water phenomena were outstanding. So, the name of these falls may originate from the Pilgrim and Puritan era. It is the name given to a place where the devil's work can be witnessed.

It is the last of a series of gorges that occur along the Bear River in Grafton Notch in Newry. There are outstanding pieces of hydraulic sculpturing here. The upstream set of falls occur where the Bear Brook splits, while passing a small island of ledge and drops three feet on either side. Downstream, the river squeezes into a narrow channel and there is a set of falls that drop two feet and leads into a section of the gorge with flat vertical walls ten feet high. The plunge pool at the bottom seems exceedingly deep.

There are wooden stairs here for re-climbing to the top of the gorge wall, so it appears that people do jump off the walls of the gorge.

⚠ **Author Note:** This could be a very dangerous, perhaps even fatal. Do not attempt.

Further downstream, the river again squeezes into a narrow channel, this time by a ledge outcropping that rises ten feet above the water line.

Here, there is a three-foot waterfall. The outcropping ends abruptly and after a dramatic gap of fifteen feet, completes a horseshoe shape, now forming the ledge wall of the river. An outstanding example of hydraulic sculpturing, the site is located at a fault line. The bedrock is sandstone interbedded with pelite or impure limestone. It was listed in editions of the Appalachian Trail Guide in the 1950s, but not in recent editions, perhaps due to the dangerous conditions of jumping off the gorge.

Waterfall Ratings

Dunn Falls
(Also known as Dunns Falls)

Directions: Route 2 South. Take ME 201 to ME 156 to US 2 W to ME 17 to ME 120. Take Newton Street to Upton Street to East B Hill Road.

The fragrant Cliff-fern grows in the steep granite cliffs of this waterfall, located on the West Branch of the Ellis River in Andover and the North Surplus Township. These falls are part of the Appalachian Trail and are a series of five falls. Of the two main falls, the upper is a fifty-foot drop, and the lower is larger, an eighty-five-foot total drop in two sections. They are horsetails and fan waterfalls. These are usually the only falls seen by visitors, because there are no trails to the other falls.

In Dunn Notch, there are four lesser falls. If the visitor does want to see these falls, the first set of lesser falls, or the upper falls is a twelve-foot total drop, which is a pitch, then a chute, then back to a pitch. Next, is a vertical ten-foot plunge set of falls into a pool. The third set of lesser falls is a plunge falls off a steep granite wall.

There is a thirty-two foot vertical fall followed by a steeply inclined broken pitch of ten feet. The last lesser falls are above this set of falls with a six-foot pitch.

There is a logging tote road that goes to the lower falls, and there are remains of a bridge at the upper falls. The bridge was most likely built during the logging era to help get supplies across the gorge to the men working in the forests.

Waterfall Ratings

Edes Falls

Directions: I-95 to exit 75. Take US 202 to ME 122 to ME 26 to ME 11. Turn right on Edes Falls Road.

Here drops another haunted waterfall discussed in this book. (The first was in Aroostook County!) These falls are on the Crooked River in Otisfield. The first European settler to this site was named Pierce. The first mill was built here in late 1700s. These falls are small pitches about a one-foot drop each. There are remnants of a dam still here, but the river now flows over the dam. There was a covered bridge here that was lost in the 1930 flood.

The first name of who built the first dam here differs—it was either Thomas or Robert Edes who built a stone dam in the late nineteenth century. At the time of the American Revolution, a feud developed in the village of Edes Mills, near the falls, between George Pierce and John McIntosh. The feud came to a head, when McIntosh became interested in Pierce's nineteen-year-old daughter. During a fight at the falls, Pierce is said to have struck McIntosh with a wooden mallet. McIntosh's ghost has been seen ever since at the falls and in the mills that were on this site. The ghost was said to open mill gates and set the machinery to operate when no one was there. The falls are a good fishing spot for landlocked salmon and the fishermen say that McIntosh's ghost is still in the area playing tricks.

Waterfall Ratings

Ellis Falls

Directions: Route 2 South. Take ME 201 to ME 201A to ME US 2W to ME 17 to ME 120, which becomes Newton Street.

The Native Americans have numerous legends about waterfalls, and this one is no exception located on the Ellis River in Andover. These are considered tiered, horsetail, and cascade falls. There is a total drop of twenty-five feet. The water is dark due to the decaying vegetation that surrounds the fall site. When the water is high, there appears to be only one fall, but when the water is low, block falls appear on top, each five foot tall and five foot wide. The bottom pitch is divided into three parallel vertical columns and a fourth broken, curved slide. The bedrock is granite with muscovite and tonalite.

There is a Native American legend here. In the legend it is called Ellis Cascade. There are two young lovers who want to be together, but the Sagamore or chief had other plans for his daughter. Because he did not want to be considered unfair, he decided that a contest would declare the winner. There was to be an archery contest at fifty paces. Luckily, the lover won his sweetheart. The loser was very unhappy, so he stole the woman and ran into the woods. When it became obvious that he was going to be caught, he forced her to jump into the falls with him, and they both died. The place is said to be haunted to this day.

Waterfall Ratings

Hiram Falls

(Also known as Great Falls; Hiram Falls Dam)

Directions: I-95 to exit 63. Take US 202 to ME 115 to ME 35. Take right onto Bridge Street, which becomes River Road.

The Bible inspired some names in Maine and one is on the Saco River in Hiram. This area is either named to commemorate the biblical town, which supplied great quantities of timber to King Solomon or it was named for the biblical King Hiram of Tyre. These falls are an eighty-foot drop in a series of cascades that have developed on the different weathering of several dikes. The water has no color or odor. There is a fault line at this site. The bedrock is interbedded pelite, limestone, and dolorite.

This was considered the worst of the falls by the river runners during the log drives. There were really two sets of falls here. The first set was called Hiram Falls, but the lower set was not so high and considered a companion to Hiram Falls, called The Wife or the Great Wife Falls.

There is a power station here that was built in 1917, and is an excellent example of an early hydroelectric station. Due to the dams in Saco and Biddeford, there are no longer runs of Atlantic salmon, shad, and alewives to these falls. However, the area does stock brown trout. The trout caught usually are in the range of eight to ten inches. It is also a well-known canoe portage site.

Waterfall Ratings

Kees Falls
(Also known as Morrison Brook Falls)

Directions: Route 2 South. Take ME 201 to ME 201A to US 2W to ME 108. Turn left onto Evans Notch Road (ME-113). Portions may be closed seasonally. There is a 2.5 mile hike to the destination.

These are considered rare falls in Maine because they suspend over the lip of the ledge before falling. Because of the second name of these falls, it is obvious that the site is on Morrison Brook in Batchelders Grant Township. These falls have a vertical plunge of twenty-five feet. This rare sight can be seen while hiking on the Highwater Trail.

Waterfall Ratings

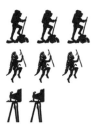

Little Boy Falls
(Also known as Parmachenee Falls)

Directions: Route 2 South. Take ME 201 to ME 201A to ME 27 to ME 4 to ME 16. Right to Morton Cutoff Road, left E Fanjoy Road, right W Fanjoy Road, right Cupsuptic Tote Road, right Lincoln Pond Road, left Greentop Road, right to Parmachenee Road (Portions unpaved).

Waterfalls are beautiful, yet very dangerous places, even today. These falls are located on the Magalloway River in Township 5, Range 5, about seven miles from the Canadian border. Folklore states that the name comes from the fact that a little Native American boy fell over the falls in a raft and died. Parmachenee is an Abenaki word that means "across the usual path."

Today, the falls are a single pitch of two to six feet, located north of Parmachenee Lake. In 1861, various publications reported that it was a fifteen- to twenty-foot drop. It was also reported that there were a lot of bugs here (though in any area where there is clean air and water, there will also be lots of bugs) and the shore was filled with decaying logs. There was also an old growth of alder trees all along the shore here.

The pool below the falls is a great trout fishing spot, said to yield eight- to twelve-inch fish, and sometimes even two pounders. President Dwight D. Eisenhower once fished here. There is a plaque imbedded in nearby rocks which states:

> "This marks the area where President Dwight D. Eisenhower fished in June 1955 – erected by the Maine Federation of Republican Women 1970."

Waterfall Ratings

Mad River Falls

Directions: Route 2 South. Take ME 201 to ME 201A to ME US 2 W to ME 108. Take left onto Evans Notch Road (ME - 113).

The name may come from its "mad" or very fast and crazy, water flow. It could also be a corruption of an Abenaki word, meaning "bad, useless river." These falls are located on the Mad River in Evans Notch. There are six horsetail falls here with a 100-foot total drop. The water is yellow-tinted in the pool at the bottom. The upper cascade is a thirteen-foot, fan-shaped drop—a three-foot drop on the top and a ten-foot drop on the bottom. The second set of falls is a narrow chute that is two feet wide, and drops twelve feet into a small pool. From the pool, the water drops three feet to enter a small basin, and then goes to the third set of falls. This set is a two-foot-wide fall with a drop of eight feet into another pool.

The fourth and fifth sets of falls are the most photogenic. The fourth falls are a vertical slide over a moss ledge fanning out as it falls. The water collects in pool, and then exits to the fifth falls. This set has a total thirteen-foot drop. It arches clockwise and fans slightly as it falls. At the bottom, is a plunge pool. The sixth set of falls is a thirty-five foot drop. This is a narrow column of water that is nearly vertical, but broken and angular in the center. The bedrock is sulfuric, carbonaceous pelite. This is an exceptional example of a mountain stream type of falls and can be found on the Royce Trail.

Waterfall Ratings

Mahoosic Notch Falls

Directions: Route 2 South. Take ME 201 to ME 201A to ME 4 to ME 108 to ME 26. Turn left onto Cable Road (portions unpaved). Turn left onto Sucker Brook Road (portions unpaved in New Hampshire). Turn left (back in Maine) and stay straight onto Success Pond Road. There is a .9 difference from road to site.

This could be a Native American historical place. The name may come from two sources. The first is Abenaki, meaning "home of hungry animals." This refers to the Monhegan-Pequot refugees, who fled from Connecticut to Maine following the Pequot War in 1637. The second source may be Natick, meaning "pinnacle." These falls are on an unnamed tributary of Bull Branch in Grafton Township.

The area is a large extended run of slides and cascades on a small mountain brook that drains Mahoosic Notch. The Appalachian Trail crosses here and is considered one of the toughest one-mile stretches on the hike.

These falls are interesting because they drop at a steep pitch fifty-degree angle, virtually without interruption for at least two hundred feet. However, no one section is vertical. This makes it difficult to ascertain height. It is a continuous, steeply inclined drop, which ranks it among the longest falls in the state, but it has no substantial vertical pitch. It does seem like a great place to hide or to retreat from an enemy.

Waterfall Ratings

Mother Walker Falls

Directions: Route 2 South. Take ME 201 to ME 201A to US 2W to ME 108 to ME 26. Turn right onto Bear River Road.

Rare sea green Chrysoberyl crystals were found on the Bear River in Grafton Notch State Park. There is a natural stone bridge and the waterfall is in the "cave" formed between the gorge walls and a huge talus boulder. This V-shaped gorge about 1,000 feet long and 43.6 feet deep. These falls are located three quarters of a mile from Screw Auger Falls. There are four waterfalls here, each about five to eight feet in height. They are a series of cascades with a total drop of ninety-eight feet. A carriage road once crossed the Bear River above the gorge. The falls are named for one of the last homesteaders to arrive in this area during the 1880s, who was called Mother Walker.

This place is composed on granite bedrock that was created by glacial melt water about 14,000 years ago. The gorge is cut between two different types of bedrock. Both glacial and postglacial stream erosion exploited faults or other structural weaknesses in the rock that may have formed the bedrock.

Mother Walker Falls. Rare sea green Chrysoberyl crystals were found here located in the Bear River in Grafton Notch State Park. There is a natural stone bridge and the waterfall is in the "cave" formed between the gorge walls and a huge talus boulder.

Rumford Falls

(Also known as Pennacook Falls; Pennycook Falls; New Pennecook Falls; Knapps Pitch; Amoscoggan Falls; Great Androscoggin Falls; New Pennycook Falls; Old Rumford Dam)

Directions: Route 2 South. Take ME 201 to ME 201A to US 2W to ME 108 into Rumford.

Another Niagara Falls reference is found at these falls, except that these falls also sometimes flow backward. The falls are located on the Androscoggin River in Rumford and claimed to be the highest falls east of Niagara. One of the names of the falls comes from the fact that the town was originally called New Pennycook. It was named after Pennycook, New Hampshire, where the early settlers came from. The name Rumford comes from Sir Benjamin Thompson, Count of Rumford, who owned most of this property at one time. In 1833, a stone flume was built at the head of the fall to divert a portion of the water to the mill. Nathan Knapp, one of the owners, stepped on the wall to see if was high enough, and as the thirty feet of water passed over the flume, he fell to the base of the falls and drowned. It is named Knapps Pitch for that reason.

Today, the falls are sometimes dry. In the 1800s, this was considered the greatest cataract in all New England. During that time, there were five pitches, but it is thought that in ancient times the descent must have been much higher. There were large holes peculiar to the falls area that were found high in the rocky banks. The whole pitch was about 176 feet long ago. In 1883, there was a reported one hundred and sixty-three foot drop.

Sometimes the falls seemed to actually flow backward. When the Magalloway River rose, it flowed into the Androscoggin River, causing it to rise. So, the water would actually run back into the Umbagog Lake for two miles, creating the appearance that it was running backward.

These were natural cascade falls. The Anasagunticook tribe lived in area, part of East Abenaki group. They came to the falls to fish for migrating Atlantic Salmon, which has been gone from here since 1817 due to other dams being built along the river. The salmon were speared while they tried to migrate up these falls, which was impossible to do. The Native American, Pierpole, stated the last time Atlantic Salmon was seen at these falls was in the late 1600s. The fish would be taken out of the thirteen-acre pool that used to be here. The gathering place to spear the salmon for the Native Americans is now the parking lot for the Rumford Information Booth. There were signs of numerous carrying places here since ancient times.

In 1890, hundreds of logs were trapped by the falls during low water. This was why and when it was decided to build the dam. This place was considered one of the greatest natural waterpowers in New England.

There are many minerals found here. Pyrite and Sahlite were found. The first report of this mineral found in Maine was here in 1837. They were dark green cleavages. Sahlite is the same as Diopside. Diopside is an important rock-forming mineral. It is also found in iron meteorites. Diopside is the magnesium rich part of a series which hedenbergite is the iron rich part. The color is clear, white, pale green to yellowish-greenish brown. If the mineral rutile is in this mineral then the diopside becomes even more valuable. If it's green, the rutile may create a "cat's eye" type of gemstone. If the color is dark, which includes rutile needles, and is aligned correctly, it can create a four-rayed star called star diopside.

Yellow garnets have also been found here. These color crystals have special properties that are said to cure jaundice. They could be part of the Grossular garnet group. The yellow color has not been named. The bedrock is pegmatite with a purplish to rusty brown color.

In 1992, this site was added to the National Registry of Historic Places. The period of significance is 8999 B.C. to 1500 A.D.

Waterfall Ratings

Directions: Route 2 South. Take ME 201 to ME 201A to US 2W to ME 108 to ME 26. Turn right onto Bear River Road.

These unique falls are one of only two falls of this type found in Maine. The other is Mother Walker Falls, discussed earlier in the chapter. These falls are on the Bear River in Grafton Township in Grafton Notch State Park. This site is named for the small round holes at the foot of the falls, which appear to be augured. The gorge has a natural bridge that is composed of granite bedrock.

The first set of falls is a thirty-five foot plunge over a lip of granite into the gorge. It is a cascade fall site with a couple of ten-foot vertical drops. The second set of falls is a three-foot drop into a punchbowl formation on top. The falls have cut a twisting gorge through grandoiorite and mica granite. The gorge is known for its intricate, tortuous shape, which is 130 feet long. Grandoiorite is the most common intrusive igneous rock. Its essential components include quartz, feldspars, hornblende and biotite. They may have been formed by glacial stream incision or during the last stages of de-glaciation, which is similar to the other gorges in this area.

There was a lumber mill built on top of the falls in 1850. It is said that the spiral waterfall was much larger during this time. Lumberjacks blasted part of the waterfall to ease the passage of logs through the gorge.

This is truly a magical place and well worth a visit. It was said that in 1861, the water was so clear here that one could see each individual pebble on the bottom of the falls.

Waterfall Ratings

Screw Auger Falls. This site is named for the small round holes at the foot of the falls, which appear to be augured.

Snow Falls

(Also known as Snow Falls Gorge)

Directions: I-95 to exit 109B. Take ME 133 W to ME 219 to ME 26.

When visiting here, it comes as no surprise that the Native Americans also have a legend about the Little Androscoggin River in West Paris. It is said to be cursed. The gorge is thirty-three feet in height and the falls flow over an eighteen-foot vertical drop at the head of the gorge. These are cascade falls and the water is slightly brown, but odorless. The bedrock is granite, and there is outstanding hydraulic sculpturing in area.

Before the dams were built on the lower Androscoggin River, Atlantic Salmon swam as far inland as Snow Falls and was used as spawning grounds. There is a bridge across the gorge and ruins of an old mill foundation found here.

There has been Salmon quartz, garnet, Black Tourmaline (Schorl), Feldspar, Muscovite (white mica crystals), Vesuvianite, and a forty-pound crystal of Rose Quartz found here. Quartz, in general, is said to create a high level of energy, even causing spiritual energy to increase. It is said that the Incas of Peru used quartz to build their temples for this very reason. It is considered a very important mineral. Rose Quartz is a pink to reddish pink variety and Salmon Quartz is a gray-colored mineral. Muscovite, or white mica, has also been found.

This area has many abandoned mines and is also cursed. The famous Molly Ockett, who was part of Pequakeet tribe, is said to have cursed this place. She was called Androscoggin Valley's Florence Nightingale. The legend states that she was born Molly Susup in Fryeburg in the 1700s. During her travels from Andover to Paris, she wanted refuge at an inn at the falls. She was refused, so she cursed the innkeeper and the whole settlement, saying that they would be short of life and none of their work, or their children's work, would prosper. No businesses are said to have prospered here since, including inns, cabins, schoolhouses, and restaurants.

The falls were actually named for Captain Snow, who was slain at the laocation by the Native Americans. He was said to camp near the falls and trapped animals there. This did not please the Native Americans, who were doing the same, so they followed the traps, which lead them to Snow. He was killed in the struggle that ensued, as well as many Native Americans during the battle.

Waterfall Ratings

Step Falls
(Also known as Wight Brook Dam)

 Directions: Route 2 South. Take ME 201 to ME 201A to US 2W to ME 108.

Could Wight Brook in Newry in Step Falls Preserve or Wight Brook Nature Preserve really be a lost gem mine location? These falls are a series of pitches, slides and cascades. There are geological potholes here, but not very deep pools. These are natural water slides; one is an eight-foot drop that inclines at a forty-five-degree angle. The total drop is one hundred and fifty feet. The water tumbles down a series of boulders and step-like ledges in yellow tinted water. It is still considered clean to swim in and there is a trail on the right side of the falls. An old water pipe ruin is seen here. It was once used to bring water to the camps about a half a mile away.

Beryl and Pyrrhotite have been found at this location. There is also a legend of a lost gem andalusite mine and quarry in the area. Green and blue tourmaline has been found on top of the falls. The ledge is composed of biotite, hornblende-biotite quartz, diorite, grandionite, and mica granite. The bedrock is granite with numerous pegmatite pods. Some of these pods are five feet across.

Waterfall Ratings

Swans Falls

(Also known as Swans Falls Dam)

Directions: I-95 to exit 63. Take ME 202 to ME 4—first exit onto US 302. Take ME 5, left onto Swan Falls Road.

At one time, the Native Americans would run these falls in their birch bark canoes, but the dam on the Saco River in the Fryeburg area makes that impossible today. The falls are named for Caleb and Dorothy Swan, who settled here, because the high water in 1766 prevented them from crossing the river to the lot that they really wanted. It is a rapid pitch of eight feet. There is an Appalachian Club Camp here. The first bridge across the Saco River was built in 1790 on this site. There was a grist mill here in 1837, but was washed away by floodwaters. During the logging era, when the loggers came to this first set of falls, they knew that things would just get worse as they continued driving the logs downriver. This was not a welcome sight to them.

The Native Americans used this place as a portage that avoided the winding part of the Saco River, called the Old Course of the Saco. The Fryeburg Canal Project, proposed in 1815 to 1836, actually altered the course of the river forever, so the carry or old portage site was no longer needed.

Waterfall Ratings

The Cataracts

Directions: Route 2 South. Take ME 201 to ME 201A to US 2W to ME 17 to ME 120. There is a .3 difference from road to site.

The water found on Frye Brook in Andover West Surplus near Grafton Notch State Park is perfectly clear and the pools below have an emerald appearance. There are three falls here with a total drop of ninety feet. During the wet season, this site becomes a series of raging cascades. The lower drop is called the "Churn," which is a fifty-foot plunge into a deep gorge. The middle falls are called, "Cataracts," which is a fifteen-foot sliding cascade. The upper falls are called, "The Flume," which is a twenty-foot drop. The waterfalls occur as the brook descends from Frye Mountain. The Appalachian Trail passes directly by these falls.

Waterfall Ratings

The Falls

(Also known as Webb River Falls; Webb River Whitewater Rapids)

 Directions: Route 2 South. Take ME 201 to ME 201A to US 2W to ME 142. Take left onto Falls Road.

This spot is found on the Webb River in Dixfield and Mexico area. Most of this river is inaccessible by road, but to the lucky visitor, the falls can actually be seen from the road. This is a set of cascades with a total drop of twenty-nine feet. During high water volume, this site has the appearance of a single vertical pitch of eight to ten feet.

Waterfall Ratings

Penobscot County

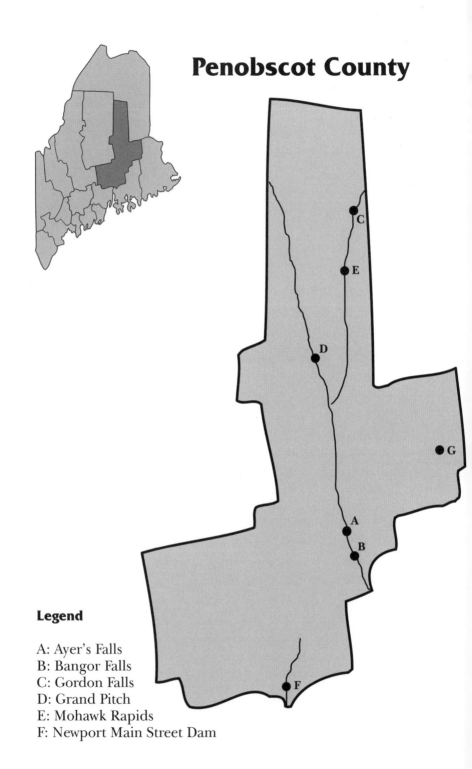

Legend

A: Ayer's Falls
B: Bangor Falls
C: Gordon Falls
D: Grand Pitch
E: Mohawk Rapids
F: Newport Main Street Dam

CHAPTER ELEVEN

Penobscot County

Today, rafters call this river the "place of river gods." The Penobscot River is an Abenaki word that means, "the rocky place" or "the descending ledge place." There was about ten miles of falls in close succession on this river that started at Treat' s Falls and ended at Old Town Falls. The Abenaki had a different word for various parts of the river. The South Branch of the Penobscot was called Onzwazagehsuck, the North Branch was called, Abacadneticook, and the East Branch was called, Wassasegewick.

No dams were built here until the 1880s, and that was basically because of the log drives. Bangor was the main place that the northern lumber companies would send their logs. When Henry Thoreau made his famous trek through this area, he was told by his Native American guide that the river once ran both ways, one half up and the other down. But since the Europeans came, and built dams, the river all runs down, and it was difficult to canoe upstream. What is interesting about this remark is that until the dams were built on this river, the Native Americans could run this river either way in their canoes.

Ayer's Falls
(Also known as Nalumsunkhungan Falls; Nerumsuckhungon Falls; Ayers Rips)

Directions: I-95 to exit 191, turn right onto Kelley Road, then left onto Main Street.

This is a Native American legend place. These rips are located on the West Branch of the Penobscot River in Orono at the mouth of the Stillwater River between Ayer's Island and Orono. The rapids are created between the rocks around the island and the bank of the river. The river drops ten feet over these rapids.

There is an unusual tale about this area. It states that this was called Nutskamongan, and it was here that the Wanagemeswak, or dwarf people, told the Abenaki that the Mohawks were coming to destroy them. These little people stayed in the woods and wore a red cap, with ears that stuck up. There are many Native American stories in Maine about little people, who lived in the woods. These people in particular were considered strange little people, though they were usually benevolent. They could, however, be very mean if laughed at. They were believed to possess the "evil eye." If they made direct eye contact with a human, it would result in immediate death or fatal illness. They were said to be about three feet high and extremely ugly.

Waterfall Ratings

Bangor Falls

(Also known as Treat's Falls; Bangor Dam)

Directions: I- 95 to exit 183. Take State Street to Bangor Water Treatment Plant next to Eastern Maine Medical Center, across from Cascade Park.

This site is located on the Penobscot River in Bangor. It was named in 1800 for the first postmaster in the area, Major Joseph Treat. Breached in 1976, it was never rebuilt. The current spirals into the historic Bangor salmon pool. When the first settlers came to this place, they found staggering amounts of fish here. The dams that were built during the log drives, dramatically reduced the fish population. The breaching of this dam, however, helped the salmon return to the Penobscot River. By 2005, eighty-one percent of all the salmon that were found in Maine rivers were found here.

Waterfall Ratings

Big Ambejackmackamus Falls
(Also known as Gulliver Pitch; Big A)

 Directions: I -95 to exit 244. Take ME 157 W, right onto Katahdin Avenue, which becomes Bates Street. Bates Street becomes Millinocket Road (portions unpaved). Take left onto Golden Road, then left onto Grant Brook Road. There is a .3 mile difference from road to destination.

The Penobscot River is one of the best whitewater rafting rivers in Maine. These waterfalls are located on the West Branch of the Penobscot in Township 3, Range 11; they drop for four miles and contain pothole hydraulics, also called keepers. This site is an important nursery for landlocked Salmon. The bedrock of rapids contains evidence of a contact zone between quartz monzonite and the northwest end of an elongated stretch of quartz diorite. Quartz diorite is used for building purposes, and contains lime-soda feldspar, quartz, hornblende, and biotite.

Ambejackmackamus is a Native American word, meaning "slant-wise of the regular route," which probably refers to the sharp S-turn the river takes. In the logging era, these falls were known as Gulliver Pitch, after a lumberjack who drowned here. Though the history of logging is exciting to read about, logging was a very dangerous job. There are numerous stories about the unlucky logger who lost his life on the Maine rivers.

Waterfall Ratings

Dexter Falls

(Also known as Dexter Grist Mill Falls)

Directions: I-95 to exit 157. Take ME 7 into downtown Dexter. Grist Mill is on left.

The East Branch of the Sebasticook River in Dexter is a spring fed river, so the water is cool and was considered clean. In 1975, the Grist Mill was added to the National Registry of Historic Places. The period of significance is 1825 to 1899. The first mill was built in 1802 and operated until 1967. The area is actually sixteen different falls, with a total drop of 1,604 feet. It is better classified as a long series of rapids.

Waterfall Ratings

Gilman Falls

(Also known as Gilman Dam; Coopers Falls)

Directions: I- 95 to exit 264. Take ME 158 to ME 11, straight on Swift Brook Road (portions unpaved). Take left onto Sherman Lumber Road (portions unpaved). Stay straight until Lunksoos Road (portions unpaved). There is a 3.7 mile walk from road to site.

The falls are bedrock sill dams with standing water that deposited fine sand on the Stillwater River in Old Town. There was a covered bridge here, the type of the bridge is unknown or unrecorded, but it did span 325 feet. It was removed in 1919.

This site seems to have been a quarry and manufacturing site between 7300-6300 years B.P. The rocks quarried here were used as long rods that were placed in the local cemeteries for some reason by the Native Americans during the Holocene era.

Waterfall Ratings

Gordon Falls
(Also known as Gordon Whitewater Rapids)

 Directions: I-95 to exit 227. Take ME 116, turn right onto Bridge Street. Turn left on US 2, turn right onto River Road.

This was a major obstacle during the log-driving era. Today, it is a portage site. This site is located on the Mattawamkeag River in the Winn area. The name was for John Gordon who built the first mill here. The Native Americans burned this mill in 1812. Another source states that a person named Gordon drowned here. Exactly who this Gordon was is unclear.

The rapids extend for a considerable distance along the river. There are also upper and lower falls. These falls are two narrow chutes, with a steep gradient and three- to four-foot standing waves. Both falls drop over vertical bedrock ledges. The ledge has been carved into potholes. This is a habitat for Atlantic Salmon and a good fishing spot for brook trout.

Serpentine and quartz have been found here. Serpentine is an adjective that means serpent-like. It has long been thought that people who carry anything made from the mineral serpentine have protection from snakebites. However, it is more likely that the mineral was named, because the colors and patterns of some of the dark green mottled crystals resemble the skins of snakes.

Waterfall Ratings

Directions: I- 95 to exit 264. Take ME 158 to ME 11 to ME 159 (portions unpaved — Shin Pond Road). Shin Pond Road becomes Grand Lake Road. Right to Scraggly Lake Road (portions unpaved). Turn left, turn right onto Huber Road (all unpaved). There is a .7 mile hike to the site.

This is a great large river fall site located on the East Branch of the Penobscot River in Township 5, Range 8. It is the third part of the Grand Pitch Formation. The river flow is exceedingly rapid and rocky here and the location is deep in the Maine north woods.

It is a rare horseshoe-shaped falls that drops almost thirty feet. Some visitors consider it a spiritual site. This slate falls site drops at right angles to vertical bedrock.

There is a well-known portage trail in area used since prehistoric times. During his trips through Maine, Henry Thoreau passed these falls. In Thoreau's time, this place sounded like a "thunder spout." This was a major obstacle during log driving era. It was dynamited during these times to ease the passage of logs. Today, it is said to be only a shadow of its former self.

Cambrian trace fossils, also known as the "age of Trilobites," have been found here. A question often arises that though Maine does have fossils, where are the dinosaurs? Unfortunately, there is a significant gap in Maine's fossil record from approximately 360 million years ago to about one million years ago. This gap is most likely the result of episodes of mountain building and erosion, which removed the rocks formed during this time period. Most recently, continental glaciers scoured the landscape, removing more sediment and rock.While this erosion was helpful in exposing the older, Paleozoic rocks, it completely removed all of the Mesozoic material and a large portion of the Cenozoic record. So, while it is quite likely that dinosaurs inhabited the area that eventually became Maine, their remains will probably never be found here.

Another unusual fossil find are the deep-water fossils that have been found in the Grand Pitch Formation. In the Cambrian era, the eastern part of North America ended in Vermont. Maine did not yet exist. Parts of Maine were assembled in the Ordovician when ancient land masses were accreted to North America. The word accreted means to add small pieces of land to larger land masses, so the animals lived and died elsewhere, but ended up as fossils in Maine.

Waterfall Ratings

Grindstone Falls

 Directions: I-95 to exit 244. Take ME 157 to left onto Grindstone Road. There is a .2 mile distance from road to site.

These are slate falls created by a narrow gorge found on the East Branch of the Penobscot River in Township 1, Range 7. The site is named because this is where boatmen used to grind their axes to sharpen them. These falls flow about a half a mile and contain heavy rapids and huge waves. It contains a rapid that is 270 feet in width and has exceptionally steep pitches. This rapid developed over ledge and boulders. The sharp tooth-like outcrops that cut diagonally across the river create an unusual set of rapids.

The plant, Purple Clematis, grows along the eastern riverbank here. This delicate lavender flower is currently known in only five other sites and is considered rare at the state level.

This is a nursery for brook trout and landlocked salmon. Small mouth bass can also be caught here. The Appalachian Mountain Club suggests to run this place with an empty canoe. It is a considered dangerous rapid. The bedrock is slate, shale and greywacke.

Waterfall Ratings

Haskell Rock Pitch
(Also known as Haskell Pitch)

Directions: I-95 to exit 244. Take ME 157 to ME 11 into Township 5, Range 8.

This rock site is located on the East Branch of the Penobscot River in Township 5, Range 8. There is an overgrown portage trail here, so it was obviously a hard place to canoe. These are the first falls in the area called the Grand Pitch Formation. The site is a twenty-foot pillar of rock that stands in the middle of the river. It is named for the lumberman who lost his life here during the log drives. The legend states that he managed to climb on to the rock, but was drowned when no one could get to him to help and the water eventually overwhelmed him.

This spot contains unusual hydrologic features, which include eddies, steep pitches, and standing waves. The rock is an extraordinary erosional remnant. The sharp bend in the river here is becoming an entrenched meander. That means that the channel is deepening by erosion and the river is becoming snake-like in shape. There are also Brachiopod, trilobite, and coral fossils found here. This is a good fishing spot for brook trout and landlocked salmon.

Waterfall Ratings

Howland Falls
(Also known as Howland Dam)

Directions: I-95 to exit 217. Right onto ME 6, left onto ME 116.

The Mayflower played a part in naming this site. It once existed on the Piscataquis River in the Howland area. These are drowned falls by the dam at the site. The natural falls dropped twenty feet. The falls and town itself were named for John Howland. He was washed over board when coming here on the Mayflower, but survived. He was the first agent at the Augusta trading post for the Plymouth Company.

Waterfall Ratings

Hulling Machine

Directions: I-95 to exit 244. Take ME 157 to ME 11 into Township 5, Range 8.

Logging played a large part in this history on this site. These falls are on the East Branch of the Penobscot River in Township 5, Range 8. This is the fourth set of falls in the area called the Grand Pitch Formation. It is named because, in log-driving era, the falls would remove the bark from, or hull, the logs being driven down the river. This is a violent and very turbulent location. It is extremely narrow, only twenty feet wide, with a ten- to fifteen-foot pitch that, because of narrow width, becomes a chute. These falls were developed over bedrock and are composed of gray, green, red slate, quartzite, and greywacke. It is a nursery for brook trout and landlocked salmon. It is definitely a portage area.

Waterfall Ratings

Medway Dam

Directions: I-95 to exit 244. Take ME 157 to ME 116. Turn right onto Jr. Mack Road, turn right onto Powersville Road. There is a .1 mile difference from road to site.

Medway is an old colonial word for middle. This dam is located on the West Branch of the Penobscot River in Medway, which is midway from Houlton to Bangor. It was helpful for the loggers to know exactly where they were during the logging era, so Medway was named appropriately.

Waterfall Ratings

Milford Falls

(Also known as Milford Dam; Bodwell Water Power Company Plant; Bodwell Power Plant; Bangor Hydro-electric Milford Plant)

Directions: I-95 to exit 193. Take US 2, then right onto Stillwater Avenue to Center Street in Milford.

The natural falls were formed by water flowing over ledge on the Penobscot River in Milford. The Native Americans called this area Sunkhaze. The town slogan is, "The best dam town in Maine," referring to its dam, which is located just south of the Penobscot Indian Island Reservation. The saw mill was a major site in the nineteenth century. The mill was burned in 1891, and almost burned the entire town when it went up in flames. That mill was designed by Wallace C. Johnson, who was a civil engineer and worked on projects at Niagara Falls in New York.

This place is named for the settlers who came from Milford, Massachusetts, before Maine became a state in 1820 and was still part of Massachusetts. The settlers missed their home in Massachusetts, so to ease the homesickness, they would sometimes name their new home in honor of the old home.

The Bodwell Water Company built this dam in 1905. If the dam were removed, the Penobscot River would actually change its shape with the change of the seasons and flow of the tides. In 1988, the site was added to the National Registry of Historic Places. The period of significance is 1900 to 1949.

Waterfall Ratings

Mohawk Rapids
(Also known as Cannibal Rapids)

Directions: I-95 to exit 227. Take ME 116 to Penobscot Valley Avenue. Take left onto US 2 and ME 116.

It is not believed that any cannibalism happened here on the Mattawamkeag River in the Lincoln area. Mattawamkeag is an Abenaki word that means "fishing place beyond a gravel bar," or in Malecite, "rapids at the mouth," or in Micmac, "on a sand bar."

The Native American legend that exists here starts with the ongoing war between the Penobscot and Mohawks in an ancient time. At this exact place, a battle between these two forces took place. The Mohawks were beaten by the Penobscots, who used concealed knifes and were able to kill many of the Mohawks. The Penobscots could not kill the chief of the Mohawks for a very long time. He was said to be a very strong man, and even managed to live when several war canoes attacked him. Eventually, the Penobscots prevailed against their enemies. The name Cannibal Rapids comes from the fact that the Penobscot tribe called the Mohawks, cannibals. In 1847, arrowheads were found here, so it is apparent that some event took place at the location.

Waterfall Ratings

Newport Main Street Dam

Directions: I-95 to exit 157. Take ME 100, turn right onto High Street, then left onto North Street.

Here is a prehistoric fishing area on the Sebasticook River in Newport. The dam was removed in July 2002, so the water phenomena that once occurred here, has returned. The word Sebasticook is Abenaki meaning "the shortest route." Apparently, the Native Americans also used this area as a short cut between two rivers.

Waterfall Ratings

Old Town Falls

(Also known as Waterworks Dam; Great Falls)

Directions: I-95 to exit 193. Take US 2, take right on Stillwater Ave, stay straight on Center Street to Old Town.

At one time, the Penobscot River Old Town falls were considered "the best waterpower in the United States." These falls were one mile above the

106

harbor. There was a covered bridge here built in 1830 by Isaac Damon. The 1846 flood washed out the bridge and it was never rebuilt.

Native Americans called this area Bemidjiwok, meaning "head of the tide." It was another natural stopping place for Native Americans, while they waited for the tide and could avoid carrying or poling the canoes over the rapids. The Native American village here was called Panawambske. The area was called Old Town in honor of the this village. The river dropped thirteen feet, and was a perfect place for Richard Winslow to build the first mill here in 1798.

The Waterworks Dam drowned these falls. Prior to this, these were tidal falls; present during low tide, but flooding out during high tide. The natural falls developed over a ledge extending directly across the river.

Waterfall Ratings

Pumpkin Hill Dam
(Also known as Lowell Tannery Dam)

 Directions: I-95 to exit 217. Take ME 115 to ME 118. Turn right onto Fogg Brook Road.

There has been controversy here in recent years, due to the death of the American Eel in the turbines at this Passadumkeag River in Lowell dam.

The name comes from folklore. The story is that a man lived at the foot of the hill and raised pumpkins that disappeared one night. He found them in a neighbor's barn at the top of the hill. When he confronted his neighbor, the neighbor claimed that the pumpkins must have rolled up hill. What the legend does not state is what happened after the neighbor heard that story.

Another legend of the area is that a great battle occurred between the Penobscot and Mohawk tribes in the winter of the early 1700s. It is said that the chief of the Penobscot tribe, Atum-bee-ark (which means bow and arrow) was almost killed. All the Mohawks were killed, except two. They were spared to tell the tale of the battle and of their defeat. However, they did leave without their ears. The ears were taken to give proof of the battle and to warn the Mohawks to not attack the Penobscot tribe again.

Waterfall Ratings

Quakish Dam

Directions: I-95 to exit 244. take ME 157W to ME 11. Turn right onto Poplar Street (ME-11). There is a .9 mile walk from road to site.

This dam is located on Quakish Lake in Township 3, Indian Purchase. Quakish is a Native American word. In Abenaki it means, "flooded place," and in Micmac, it means "rough strewn."

In January 1904, this was the scene of a logging incident that changed the log drives on the Penobscot River forever. Marsh and Ayer, two loggers, accused Great Northern Paper Company of delaying the log drive here, by diverting more water for its mill. Millions of lumber was lost due to ice because of the company taking the extra water. Great Northern Paper was found guilty and had to pay over $9,000 to the loggers. This court case marked the beginning of the end of the Penobscot River log drives boom of the 1800s. Less and less timber was sent down the river after this date for fear of lawsuits and the logging boom started to come to an end.

Waterfall Ratings

Slewgundy Heater
(Also known as The Heater; Slugunda Falls)

Directions: I- 95 to exit 182A. Take US1A to ME 46 to ME 9. Turn left onto CCC Road (unpaved). There is a .5 mile hike from this point to destination.

This is one of Maine's most spectacular whitewater stretches. This incredible rapid site is located on the Mattawamkeag River in Mattawamkeag. These rapids are two miles in length with well-developed potholes. The river narrows abruptly into a thirty-foot wide chute, then quickly widens. The bedrock is slate and phyllite. The rapids develop on vertically dipping bedrock ledges. Serpentine may occur here and large quartz veins have been found here. It is a habitat for Atlantic Salmon.

In the spring, the water appears to "boil" within the cauldron-like wall of the riverbanks, hence the word "heater." The name also has logging history attached. Slewgundy is an old logging word for narrow and winding course or path where log jams were likely to occur. This spot was legendary during the log driving days and considered one of the toughest tests for the river runners. Many loggers did not make it through and there were many documented drownings. The area was and should be respected as a dangerous water phenomena.

Waterfall Ratings

Stair Falls

Directions: I-95 to exit 244. Take ME 157 to ME 11 into Township 5, Range 8.

These falls occur on the East Branch of the Penobscot River in Township 5, Range 8. They are a succession of shallow ledge drops that cause rapids about an eight to twenty-four foot drop. The rapids formed over resistant rock layers, so between the number of drops and the symmetry of the rapids when viewed, it becomes an unusual rapid on the Penobscot River. Since large blocks cannot fall freely away from the lip of the bedrock, the water falls in a series of small regular drops. The drops resemble a flight of stairs going down the river, hence the name. This site contains an unusual type of bedrock. There are two types of rocks found here; sandstone on the far side of the rapid and finer sandstone toward the ledges. This is also a spawning ground for landlocked salmon and brook trout.

Waterfall Ratings

Veazie Falls

(Also known as Veazie Dam; White Water Falls; Wabenobanktuk Falls)

Directions: I-95 to exit 187. Make U-turn to US 2. Turn right on Main Street.

In 1957, experts claimed that a gold vein ran west from Veazie Falls and terminated near Stillwater. This is unsubstantiated at this time, but it is a very interesting claim.

These were Penobscot River in Veazie rapids in their natural state, but the dam that was built in 1866 at this site has drowned them today. However, in August 2008, this dam has been slated to be removed and decommissioned, so in time, the fish and rapids will return.

The Native American word, Wabenobanktuk means, "white water falls or white falls." It is thought that Maine' s famous Red Paint People may have lived and/or fished at these falls. One of their pre-historic cemeteries was found here on the east side.

Waterfall Ratings

Piscataquis County

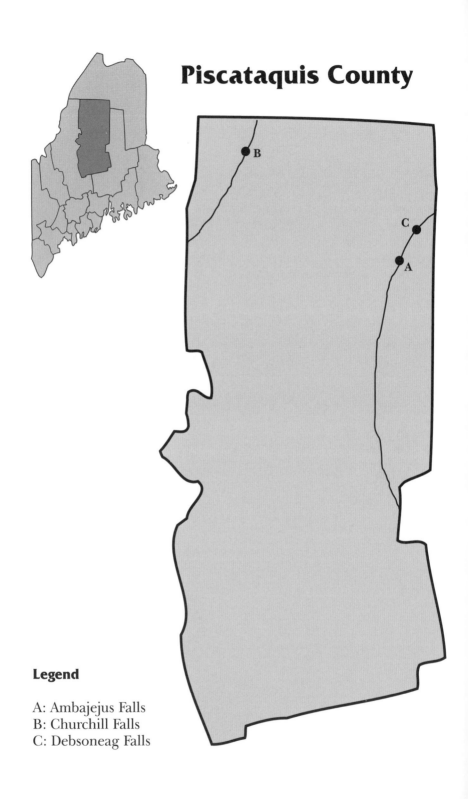

Legend

A: Ambajejus Falls
B: Churchill Falls
C: Debsoneag Falls

CHAPTER TWELVE
Piscataquis County

There are two Dennys Rivers in Maine. One is the Dennys River in Washington County and the other is the Denny's River in Piscataquis County. Notice the spelling differences. That is the only way to tell them apart, other than the actual location.

This county is larger than the state of Connecticut. The Native American word means, "rapid water." There is no doubt that this area has a lot of fast water running through it.

Abol Falls
(Also known as Little Abol Falls)

Directions: I-95 to exit 244. Take ME 157 to Katahdin Avenue to Bates Street to Millinocket Avenue to Golden Road. (Portions unpaved on all roads). Take left into Baxter Park Road. Gate access required at park. Turn left onto Park Tote Road (unpaved).

These falls are cascade waterfalls on a tributary to the West Branch of the Penobscot River on Little Abol Stream in Township 2, Range 10. The area contains a rapid with a width of 264 feet. The total drop is thirteen feet.

Abol is the shortened Abenaki word for rapids. It literally means "where the water laughs in coming down." There is another Abenaki word, Aboljecarmegus or Aboljackarnegassic, meaning "smooth ledge falls" or "bare, devoid of trees," that may mean these falls.

The mineral found here is monzonite. The ledge is composed of Katahdin granite. Katahdin Granite is a pink to gray color, the pink granite occurring toward the summit and the gray color toward the base of the mountain. This place is an important nursery for landlocked salmon and brook trout.

Abol Falls can be found hiking on the Appalachian Trail. When Henry Thoreau came through here, he saw logs piled up on the sides of the river, where there had been a huge log jam due to the flood that occurred here earlier in the year. At this time, the falls were perpendicular with a nine to ten foot drop.

Waterfall Ratings

Directions: I-95 to exit 244. Take ME 157 to Katahdin Avenue to Bates Street to Millinocket Avenue to Golden Road. (Portions unpaved on all roads). Take left into Baxter Park Road. Gate access required at park. Turn left onto Park Tote Road (unpaved). There is a 2.5 mile hike to destination.

This is a classic water slide over an extended length of smooth ledge, located on Abol Stream in Township 2, Range 10. The vertical drop is twelve feet at a thirty-degree angle. The width of the slide is twenty feet. The ledge is composed of granite. This site is located in Baxter State Park.

⚠ **Author Note:** At one time, the visitor could slide down here, but it is now highly discouraged due to the fact that two to three people per year would get seriously hurt. It is my recommendation that you do not try this.

Waterfall Ratings

Directions: I-95 to exit 244. Take ME 157 to Katahdin Avenue to Bates Street to Millinocket Avenue to Golden Road. (Portions unpaved on all roads). Take left into Baxter Park Road. Gate access required at park. Turn left onto Park Tote Road (unpaved). There is a .3 walk from road.

The falls are drowned during high water on the West Branch of the Penobscot River in Baxter State Park in Township 1, Range 9. The name is Abenaki, meaning "two currents," or "one on either side." These are rough and broken rapids occurring between Passamagmet and Ambejejus Lakes.

Thoreau had to portage or carry around these falls when he visited the area in the 1880s. The portage was extremely difficult. It was said to be through woods, up hill at an angle of forty-five-degrees, over rocks and logs almost continuously.

There is an ancient, prehistoric campsite in the area. In 1995, this place was added to the National Registry of Historic Places. The period of significance is 999 B.C. to 500 A.D.

Waterfall Ratings

Big Niagara Falls

Directions: I-95 to exit 244. Take ME 157 to Katahdin Avenue to Bates Street to Millinocket Avenue to Golden Road. (Portions unpaved on all roads). Take left into Baxter Park Road. Gate access required at park. Turn left onto Park Tote Road (unpaved). There is a 1.7 mile hike to destination from here.

Here is another mention of Niagara Falls. These falls are located on Nesowadnehunk Stream in Baxter State Park in Township 3, Range 10. They are a seventy-foot drop, over pink and gray Katahdin granite. The name comes from some visitors thinking that there was a resemblance to Niagara Falls in New York. The main falls is a vertical drop of twenty feet, broad at the top, but compressed to half the width from the midpoint to the bottom by the ledge side walls. Hydraulic sculptures exist here, which include potholes and scour marks.

These falls are glacial in origin. Old pin holes can be found here, especially next to the main drop, where spikes were driven in to build structures to aid log driving over the falls during the log driving days. As stated earlier, the logging industry felt these waterfall sites were obstacles and they would not go around them. They would usually find a way through them or over them. Many waterfall sites were destroyed forever to make way for the logs.

Waterfall Ratings

Directions: I-95 to exit 157. Take ME 7 to ME 23 TO ME 15/ME 6. Turn right onto Elliottsville Road, left onto Mountain Road. There is a .3 mile difference from here to site.

This waterfall is located on the West Branch of the Pleasant River. It is one of Gulf Hagas' five falls and part of the Bowdoin College Grant Township. This is a plunge waterfall, one of two nearly vertical waterfalls each with twelve-foot drops, running through a 400-foot-high gorge. There are swift and dangerous currents at the bottom of these falls.

⚠ **Author Note:** In recent years, there have been people who have drowned in these falls after jumping in off the fifteen-foot ledge. This is highly dangerous stunt and is discouraged.

There are potholes and scour marks here that are found sixty feet above the present river. This evidence suggests that the falls formed during the late glacier period, or has a post-glacial origin. It was probably formed by the release of water from an ice-dammed lake to the north or by superposition through dead ice.

Logs were driven through Gulf Hagas during the logging era, but the problems they encountered with the falls were huge. There is an old hunting camp located here. Today, it is a well-known side trail off the Appalachian Trail.

Waterfall Ratings

Buttermilk Falls

Directions: I-95 to exit 157. Take ME 11 to 5 miles north of Brownville Junction. Take left at Katahdin Iron Works, travel 7 miles to gate. The visitor must register and pay a fee to enter. Bear right across the Pleasant River, turn left. Parking lot is on this road.

This is the largest drop on the West Branch of the Pleasant River in Gulf Hagas, which is part of the Bowdoin College Grant Township. It is a twenty-five-foot vertical plunge off a sheer ledge that is divided by outcroppings of the ledge into three columns. The center column has the most water flow, framed by nearly matching columns on either side. The water has a noticeably brown tint as it flows over the falls and churns turbulently in the large pool at the base. The overall effect is one of buttermilk churning, hence the name.

Loggers had a lot of difficulty driving logs through Gulf Hagas, as one could imagine by the description. The Jaws, a dramatic violent section of this gorge, has outstanding displays of hydraulic sculpturing and occurs just downstream from these falls. It is hard to imagine how any logs made it through here intact and to the mills down river, but somehow the loggers made it happen. It is proof of how dedicated and tough these men were. Presently, this is a well-traveled side trail off the Appalachian Trail.

Gulf Hagas is part of what is called the Hundred Mile Wilderness. This gorge is four miles long and has been called, the Grand Canyon of the East.

Waterfall Ratings

Churchill Falls

(Also known as Churchill Dam; Main Falls; Heron Lake Dam; Chase Carry;Chase's Rapids)

Directions: I-95 to exit 286. Take US 2 to ME 212 to ME 11. Turn left onto Garfield Road, left onto Craig Road, left onto Pinkham Road (unpaved). Turn right onto Pell and Pell Road (unpaved) and right onto Churchill Dam Road (unpaved).

The natural falls on the Allagash River in Township 10, Range 12 dropped twelve feet, and it was a portage site. These rapids are part of the Allagash Wilderness Waterway. There are nine miles of rapids, containing steep drops and three to four foot standing waves. The total drop of this site is thirty-six feet. In December 1901, this was the place where hunters had the last authenticated sighting of Maine's native caribou herd. It is also a nursery for brook trout and considered a cold water fishery.

The name has an interesting history. In the early 1800s, William Harford, William Churchill, and a son from each family, were on a moose-hunting trip around the Moosehead Lake region. While the adults were gone, the boys rowed out into the lake and the canoe tipped over, drowning Churchill's son. He was said to be buried somewhere along the shore. The name here was given in honor of William Churchill.

During the logging era, the logging companies felt that it took too long to move logs along the natural routes from the northern counties, so they decided to build a faster way to move logs. The Telos Cut was made through a natural ravine between Telos Lake and Webster Lake to speed the process. This dam was constructed in 1846 to raise the water levels in Eagle Lake and Churchill Lake to implement the Telos Canal system. The original dam was a timber crib dam. A new dam was built in 1998 that has a fish ladder to maintain the fish migration.

Waterfall Ratings

Debsoneag Falls

Directions: I-95 to exit 244. Take ME 157 W to Katahdin Avenue, which becomes Bates Street, which becomes Millinocket Road (portions unpaved). Take left onto Golden Road, then slight left onto Debsconeag Road. There is a .2 mile walk to destination.

These falls are located on the West Branch of the Penobscot River in Township 2, Range 9. The rapids are a 1,300-foot-long stretch. The name comes from the Abenaki word meaning "carrying place," or "ponds at the high place," or "ponds at the waterway." This is a good example of rapids developing over resistant rock and eroded debris. The head of the rapids are marked by large standing waves with exceptional turbulence. The bedrock is composed of medium-grained Katahdin quartz monzonite. It is an important nursery for landlocked salmon.

Since it is obvious that the Native Americans believed this was a hard place to get through (they carried their canoes around the obstacle as evidenced by the name), it comes as no surprise that this was an obstacle during the log drives. Log booms were used to collect logs until the water level was high enough to carry them over the rapids. Today, huge old logs, still chained together, are beached on the eastern bank of these falls. Today, it is usually a portage site for canoes and very difficult for rafts to go through.

Waterfall Ratings

Dover Great Falls

(Also known as Browns Mills Falls; Dover Lower Village Falls; Moosehead Manufacturing Dam; Piscataquis Falls)

Directions: I-95 to exit 157. Take ME 7 to center of Dover-Foxcroft.

This dam is located on the Piscataquis River in Dover-Foxcroft. Before the town was incorporated, it was called Township 5, Range 7. The natural falls dropped 23.5 feet, over a horizontal distance of 325 feet. Due to the building of the dam in this spot, the water flow has increased over these falls.

Waterfall Ratings

East Branch Pleasant River Falls

Directions: I-95 to exit 157. Take ME 7 to ME 15 to ME 6 to ME 11. Take right on Church Street in Brownville.

These falls are located on the East Branch of the Pleasant River in the Brownville area. It is better classified as rapids. There are actually two more pitches along the river below Ebeemee Lake. There are hydrodam remains at this place.

The visitor can see the logs that were left behind on the banks from the log-driving era. The dam has been removed, so the river has reverted back to its original form. It is in the Hobstown area, which is a ghost town today, and has been incorporated into Brownville. At one time, this town had a school, homes, and a store.

The area was first known as Township 5, Range 8NWP. In November 1879, Mr. Will Frost was fatally injured in this area while rolling logs.

Waterfall Ratings

Grand Pitch
(Also known as Grand Falls; The Main Pitch)

 Directions: I- 95 to exit 244. Take ME 157 W. Take left onto Cedar Street, then right onto Balsam Road to Baxter State Park.

These falls are considered one of the most beautiful in the state, and are located on Webster Brook in Trout Brook Township. They are twenty- to twenty-five-foot vertical waterfalls that occur in two stages in immediate succession. This is one of the few waterfalls found in Baxter State Park and there is a five-mile hike to the site.

The bedrock is interbedded pelite and sandstone. Hydraulic potholes occur here. In 1864, Thoreau was briefly separated from his guide while here, and since he was in such a remote area, he writes that it did cause him some concern. Eventually, the two found each other and the trip continued.

Waterfall Ratings

Grand Falls
(Also known as Grand Pitch)

Directions: I-95 to exit 244. Take ME 157 W. Take left onto Cedar Street, then right onto Balsam Road to Baxter State Park.

At times, the names of waterfall sites can be very confusing, and this one on Wassatequoik Stream in Baxter State Park in Township 4, Range 9, is one of those places. That is why knowing the location and not just the name of a place is so important. These are cascading falls into gorge. They are ledge drops over jointed granite. There are two pitches of twenty feet, and a number of small drops that create these fall. The falls is formed over a lag deposit and jointed bedrock. Huge jointed granite slabs have fallen off the ledge into the riverbed. The bedrock is composed of Katahdin quartz monzonite and granite. Numerous potholes occur here.

This site was dynamited during log-driving days to ease the passage of logs down the stream, so it was much larger at one time. Today, this is a fishing spot for landlocked salmon and brook trout.

Waterfall Ratings

Indian Stream Falls

Directions: I-95 to exit 157. Take ME 7 to ME 23 to ME 16 to ME 6. Take right, then left onto N Guilford Road. Right to Farm Quarry Road, right to Willimantic Road, right to Mountain Road, left to ME 150. Take left onto Earley S. Camp Road. Take the next three right turns. There is a .3 mile hike to fall site.

This site is located on Indian Stream in Elliotsville Township. Indian Stream is a tributary of Wilson Stream. The first set of falls is a vertical drop of four feet over ledge. The main falls are a near-vertical fifty-five foot plunge. These falls begin with a hanging plunge of twenty feet, then five feet into a small pool. The rest of the drop is through a narrow chute.

There is a railroad bed that passes near this site that was once the lifeline for the small communities that lived here. Until 1961, a steam train called "The Scoot" operated on this railroad. The Scoot's schedule was irregular, but its whistle always signaled the arrival. If missed, one was out of luck until it came back. Passenger service continued on this line until 1966.

Waterfall Ratings

Jo-Mary Rips
(Also known as Walker Rips)

 Directions: I-95 to exit 157. Take ME 7 to ME 15 to ME 6 to ME 11 on the way to Millinocket.

These rips are on the east branch of the Pleasant River in the Brownville area on Route #11. The name Jo-Mary comes from the Native American chief, who was well known for his hunting and swimming skills. The area is also called Moorseville Prairie, an unorganized territory in Maine. The rapids are considered Class I or II.

There is a steel bridge here today, but there was a covered bridge at one time. It is called the Walker Bridge, and is said to be haunted by a little girl from this area, who drowned in the fast water. The girl is said to be seen on the bridge by passing vehicles and even near the river. This should be a warning to all visitors that any and all water phenomena, even if the water is not falling over a ledge, should be considered dangerous and treated with respect.

Waterfall Ratings

Katahdin Stream Falls

Directions: I-95 to exit 244. Take ME 157 to Katahdin Avenue to Bates Street to Millinocket Avenue to Golden Road. (Portions unpaved on all roads). Take left into Baxter Park Road. Gate access required at park. Turn left onto Park Tote Road (unpaved). There is a 2.7 mile hike to the destination.

Another waterfall is found on Katahdin Stream in Baxter State Park on the southwest corner of Mount Katahdin in Township 3, Range 10. This is a fifty-foot total drop and a tiered waterfall. The falls consist of four vertical consecutive drops.

The bedrock is Ordovician age Katahdin granite that is well jointed. The Ordovician period was named from the ancient Celtic tribe, the Ordovices, renown for their resistance to Roman domination. British geologist Charles Lapworth named this age in 1879. This era produced lime and other carbonate rocks that accumulated in the shallow sea environment here. Quartzites were also created in this time. During this era, the earth had a milder climate and the atmosphere had a lot of moisture. It was in this time when the most volcanic activity occurred in Maine.

Waterfall Ratings

Lazy Tom Dam

Directions: I- 95 to exit 157. Take ME 7 to ME 23 to ME 6 to Lily Bay Road. This road becomes Sias Hill Road to Greenville Road. (portions unpaved). There is a .3 walk to the site.

This dam is located on Lazy Tom Pond in Township 1, Range 13. There are two stories about how this area was named, and both are folklore. The first story is that it is named for a lazy Native American logger named Tom, who lived here. The second story is that it was a brand of tobacco that was sold in Greenville. The storekeeper bought bulk tobacco and split it in two. He put some into bags that were labeled Lazy Tom and he put the rest in another labeled bag. When the loggers became tired on one kind, they would just switch to the other brand.

Waterfall Ratings

Little Wilson Falls
(Also known as Wilson Falls)

Directions: I-95 to exit 157. Take ME 7 to ME 23 to ME 6. take right onto Bob Young Road (portions unpaved). There is a .4 mile hike from here.

Nature continues to astound mere mortals. Sometimes, why some natural phenomena exists is not known or understood. These Little Wilson Stream in Elliotsville Plantation waterfalls flow over slate with a forty-foot vertical cascade drop. It can be found about two miles up a side tributary of Little Wilson Stream. This is one of tallest vertical drops in Maine. The water is slightly brown with no odor. The bedrock is slate with a nearly vertical primary cleavage.

The reason for this large falls and gorge to exist is not clear, since the axis of the canyon does not correspond to any rock structures.

There is evidence that the canyon axis corresponds to a fault and a fault line, so perhaps that is the reason they are here.

During log-driving days, logs were actually run over these falls, but they usually ended up split and quartered. Today, there are still some large, cut logs in the gorge from the remnants of those days. This can be seen while hiking and is accessible from the Appalachian Trail by a side trail.

Waterfall Ratings

Nesowadnehunk Falls

(Also known as Horseshoe Falls; Nesowadnehunk Slide; Sourdnahunk Falls;Soudyhunk Falls; Sowadnehunk Falls; Souadneunk; Nesowadnehunk Dam)

 Directions: I-95 to exit 244. Take ME 157 to Katahdin Avenue to Bates Street to Millinocket Avenue to Golden Road. (Portions unpaved on all roads).

These are one of the rare horseshoe-shaped falls found in Maine and is the seventh waterfalls located on the West Branch of the Penobscot River in Township 2, Range 10, in Baxter State Park. The block falls have a total drop of seven to twelve feet and span the entire river, where Nesowanehunk Stream meets the Penobscot River. There is a five-foot slide at the bottom of the falls. The name, Nesowadnehunk, is Abenaki, meaning "swift stream between mountains." Souadneunk is Native American word meaning "running between mountains." This is, and was, a well-known portage on the Golden Road. There is also an exceptional view of Mount Katahdin from here. Thoreau passed these falls and it is still considered a good fishing area today.

In 1870, Big Sebattis Mitchell, Chief of the Penobscot Tribe, ran these falls in a canoe with the aid of a bowman; though they were forced to bail out at the base because the canoe was sinking. When the log drivers and river runners heard this tale, they had to try it, but with much less success. There were many smashed boats, numerous rescues, and at least one drowning by those trying to imitate this feat, but were never able to.

Waterfall Ratings

Ripogenus Falls
(Also known as Ripogenus Rips; Rip Dam; Ripogenus Dam)

 Directions: I-95 to exit 244. Take ME 157 W to Katahdin Avenue to Bates Street to Millinocket Avenue to Golden Road. (Portions unpaved on all roads).

These falls are impassable for open canoes on the West Branch of the Penobscot River in Township 3, Range 11. The name is Abenaki, meaning "small rocks, gravel." These falls drop fifteen feet over pink granite and occur downstream from the dam.

Nick Norcross, who was an early logger, is said to be the first person to drive logs through here. He was also the first to furnish all his men with life preservers before they started the drive. Brachiopod fossils and coral fossils have also been found in this location. This evidence suggests that this area was once an ocean reef.

The mineral Calcite, Epidote, and Prehnite have been found as well. Epidote is not well known for producing exceptional crystals, but it can produce a unique green color, called pistachio, which is considered striking. Calcite is Calcium Carbon, which is a part of marble. It comes from the Greek word, chalix, meaning "lime." It is the most common mineral found on Earth and comprises about four percent of the width of the Earth's crust, occurring in many different geological environments. Calcite can form rocks of considerable size and constitutes a significant part of all three major rock types. It is also the primary mineral component to cave formation. Its color is variable, but generally white, colorless, and occasionally iridescent.

This dam was built in 1916 to control the water in the river for log drives. When the dam was built, it was the fourth largest dam in the United States. The water here is cool year round. In 1995, this site was added to the National Registry of Historic Places. The period of significance is 5999 B.C. to 2499 B.C.

This is the dam that actually drowned another dam built at an early time. The Chesuncook Dam is now under water. It was built around 1840 and was the first built that cost $7,000. It is the site of the Woodsmen' s Memorial today.

Waterfall Ratings

Sebec Falls
(Also known as Sebec Village Falls; Sebec Dam)

 Directions: I-95 to exit 157. Take ME 7 to ME 15 to ME 6. Turn left onto Sebec Village Road. Turn left onto Chapel Lane.

These rapids were located on the Sebec River in the center of Sebec Village. The name is Abenaki, meaning, "much water." There is a dam at this site today. This was the first town to be incorporated in 1812 in the county. However, it was part of Hancock County at the time, not Piscataquis.

Waterfall Ratings

Sourdnahunk Lake Dam
(Also known as Toll Dam)

Directions: I-95 to exit 244. Take ME 157 W to Katahdin Avenue to Bates Street to Millinocket Avenue to Golden Road. (Portions unpaved on all roads).

Tolls were needed even before highways were built in Maine. This toll site was located on the mouth of the Sourdnahunk Stream into Sourdnahunk Lake in Township 4, Range 10. In 1878, the logging companies needed to find a way to run logs through this area to get to the Penobscot River more easily. The companies petitioned the Maine legislature to allow them to construct a dam and the right to collect a toll for the passage of all logs through the dam area. The original foundation still exists though the dam has been re-built three times. The original dam was put together without any iron used. This is also the first documentation found when dynamite was was used in the woods of Maine. Though it was said that many of the waterfalls in this area were very large and loud, they must have seemed very quiet, compared to the dynamite explosions.

Waterfall Ratings

Stair Falls

Directions: I-95 to exit 157. Take ME 7 to ME 23 to ME 6. Take right onto Elliottsville Road, then turn left onto Mountain Road.

The Native American name for this site was Elandamookganopskitachwak. No exact translation is known. These falls are on the West Branch of the Pleasant River in Bowdoin College Grant Township part of the Gulf Hagas area. It is the middle fall site of the three large falls in this area. These are cascade falls that creates a stair-like look, hence the name. There is about an eighteen-foot drop to these falls; it depends on run off.

Gulf Hagas is considered to have regional significance. The potholes and scour marks here are sixty feet above the present river, suggesting that it has a late or post-glacial origin. It was probably formed by the release of water from an ice-dammed lake to the north or by superposition through dead ice. Logs were driven through the Gulf during that era, but the problems they encountered were tremendous here. It is truly amazing that any logs actually made it to the market. The obstacles were numerous and there was no easy way to complete this goal. Only through hard work and persistence did this industry thrive.This area can be found on a well-traveled side trail off the Appalachian Trail.

Waterfall Ratings

Telos Dam

Directions: I-95 to exit 244. Take 157W to Katahdin Avenue to Bates Street to Millinocket Road. Left onto Golden Road, right onto Telos Road, right onto Coffee Los Road. (Parts of all roads are unpaved). There is a .7 mile difference from road to site.

This dam is located on Telos Lake. The name is Greek, meaning, "far, ultimate, the end." The dam was built in 1841. After it was built, logs still did not move fast enough to market for the lumber companies. So, in 1842, the Telos Cut opened below the dam and the first pine logs were driven through. The Cut actually altered the Allagash Waterway, making it part of the Penobscot River drainage area.

Waterfall Ratings

The Chimney

Directions: I-95 to exit 244. Take ME 157W to Cedar Street. Turn right onto Balsam Drive to park.

This notch site is on an unnamed brook in Baxter State Park. It is a steep gorge on the south wall of the Great Basin, which is a notch between Pamola Peak and Chimney Peak. There is a little brook there that flows through a deep gash in the wall for about one and a half miles. This is a trail for experienced climbers; many people have been killed or hurt here. *Baxter State Park officials recommend that this trail not be used to climb the north face of Mount Katahdin.* It is a fully enclosed hollow area that is blocked internally by four large wedge stones, or clock stones. In the winter, this is an ice waterfall, and in the summer, if dry, it can be just a trickle, but during the high volume or wet seasons, this can become a tiered and segmented waterfall.

Waterfall Ratings

The Cribworks
(Also known as The Cribwork Whitewater Rapids)

Directions: I-95 to exit 244. Take ME 157 W to Katahdin Avenue to Bates Street to Millinocket Avenue to Golden Road. (Portions unpaved on all roads).

This rapid site is located on the West Branch of the Penobscot River in Township 3, Range 11. It is a one-mile stretch of rapids and considered one of Maine' s most turbulent rapids. This water phenomena formed over structural weakness in the bedrock and contains unusual hydrologic features that include large eddies and exceptionally steep pitches. The rapids developed on bedrock benches formed by the splitting away or sheeting of blocks off the bedrock. It is a ten-foot vertical drop with dangerous chutes, eddies, and large boulder piles all through it. There are also well-developed potholes that have formed on the bedrock of Katahdin Quartz monzonite. The lower section of the site is comprised of eroded debris. There are five- to six-foot standing waves and the large eddies created by the irregular riverbed resemble a giant cauldron.

The log drives are probably where this place got its name. A certain type of dam was erected here. An old stone and wood "cribwork" dam can be seen on the northern end of the rapid. This dam was used to block off a small side channel and augment the water flow of the main stream. This flooded out natural obstacles, and also funneled the logs into the main branch of the river. There are the remains of an ancient campsite here and today this site is an important nursery for landlocked salmon.

Waterfall Ratings

Trafton Falls

Directions: I-95 to exit 157. Take ME 7 to ME 15 to ME 16 to ME 11. Follow this route into the center of Milo.

This site was located on the Sebec River in the center of Milo. Milo was first called Plantation #3, Seventh Range. The natural falls had a total drop of fourteen feet, and there is a dam at the site today. The first saw and grist mill was built here in 1823 by Captain Winborll A. Sweat.

The name of the falls comes from Mark Trafton, who was running the falls on a raft and was thrown overboard. He was rescued and saved, but only with great difficulty.

Waterfall Ratings

Tumbledown Dick Stream Falls

Directions: I-95 to exit 157. Take ME 7 to ME 15 to ME 16 to ME 11. Turn left onto Fire Road 3/ Turkeytail Road (portions unpaved). There is a .2 mile walk to site.

These are mountain top waterfalls and it is very unusual for falls like this to occur in Maine. The flow is located on Tumbledown Dick Stream in Township 1, Range 11. The main falls are a sixty-foot vertical drop from the top to the bottom, but a break in between makes this a chute fall. At the base of the fall, is a shallow pool, completely enclosed on east and west side by granite cliffs sixty to one hundred feet high. These are the only falls that support high-altitude vegetation that includes, lichen, low bush blueberries, and small shrubs.

Gold, emerald beryl, garnet, smoky quartz, mica, and purpurite have been found here. Purpurite is a Manganese Phosphate and forms a series with heterosite. Purpurite is the manganese rich part and heterosite is the iron rich part. These are very uncommon minerals, and are considered valuable because of its purple color and rarity.

Waterfall Ratings

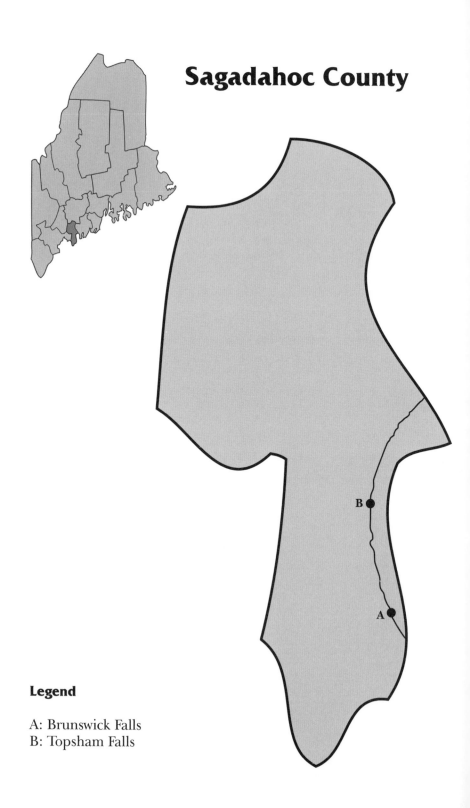

Sagadahoc County

Legend

A: Brunswick Falls
B: Topsham Falls

CHAPTER THIRTEEN

Sagadahoc County

Sagadahoc is a Native American word, meaning "mouth of big river" or "the out flowing of the swift stream as it nears the sea."

Brunswick Falls

(Also known as also known as Androscoggin River Falls; Androscoggan Falls)

 Directions: I-95 to exit 103. Take ME 196S via exit 31A toward Brunswick. Turn right onto US 201.

Here is another example of very unusual natural phenomena. These falls are located on the Androscoggin River in the Brunswick area and were block falls with a 41-foot single drop running for 1,980 feet. The first saw mill was established here in 1717. This was the center of the "ancient region of pejepscot." It was called Pejepscot after the Native Americans who lived in the seasonal villages along the falls. The Native Americans living here before the Eurpoeans arrived actually had a large fort and may have conspired to exterminate the English who settled in the area.

Something cataclysmic happened to the land forms in the geologic past. The Androscoggin River runs southeast toward the sea until it hits a wall at Topsham. There it takes a left, goes over these falls, and heads upcountry (or so it seems) to Merrymeeting Bay. Why this happens is not known. There is a plant at this site superimposed on the natural falls today. This site is at the mouth of the Androscoggin, so the dam is the one that stopped the natural fish migration on the river. Below the falls, there are excellent fishing grounds where one could catch striped bass, white perch, sea-run brown trout, brook trout, and the occasional Atlantic Salmon.

There has been a drowning here. Before 1820, Major Burt Townsend and a Mr. Gross were on a raft of logs just above these falls, when the raft broke loose and went over the falls. Major Townsend leaped into the river and did not go over, but Mr. Gross drowned after going over the falls.

The natural rocks in the falls show garnets, green felspar, and quartz. Ferrimolybdite has been found here, just below the bridge and very close to the water's edge. This mineral is a yellow color. Molybdenite, gunmetal blue crystals, has also been found on the banks of the river. Molybdenite, also known as Moly Ore, is a very soft metallic mineral. It is usually confused with graphite, but is more bluish-silver in color. It is soft enough to be used to leave marks on paper and feels very greasy because of its extreme softness.

Almandine or large garnets, up to 25 cm, were found here in 1958. Almandine is the aluminum garnet and is fairly common. It is usually found in mica rocks. Pure Almandine is rare in nature. It comes red to brown in color.

Muscovite and Microcline have been found. Feldspar is the most common mineral in granite. Muscovite is a common rock-forming mineral. It is not considered valuable by itself, but it often accompanies valuable minerals, such as topaz, beryl, and almandine. The sheets of this mineral are flexible and elastic; they can be bent and will flex back to original shape. The color is silvery to amber.

Smoky Quartz has been discovered. Quartz, in general, is said to create a high level of energy, even causing spiritual energy to increase. It is considered a very important mineral. Smoky Quartz is a brown to gray variety.

Monazite is another mineral that has been found here. This mineral acts as a repository of rare earth minerals and is brown in color. Monazite is really three different minerals technically, but there is no major difference between them, so they are referred to as one mineral. The Greek word, monazein, means "to be alone." These minerals form as solitary crystals. Monazite is the primary ore of several rare Earth metals; thorium, cerium, and lanthanum. All these metals are rare and quite valuable. Thorium is radioactive and could be used as a replacement for uranium. Monazite is sometimes highly radioactive. Crystals of this mineral are durable and are weathered out from their host rocks and carried downstream great distances to usually collect in river bottoms or at fall sites. Their great density makes it easy for the crystals to be collected into placer deposits. Placers are deposits where heavier objects settle, while the force of water constantly removes lighter objects. Valuable ores, like rutile and monazite; or metals, like gold and platinum; or gemstones, like diamonds, rubies, and sapphires, can all be found in placer locations.

Waterfall Ratings

The Chops

Directions: I-95 to exit 103. Take I-295 to exit 43. Take sharp left onto ME 197 to ME 24 to ME 128. Take right onto Chopps Point Road.

This extinct waterfall site is on Merrymeeting Bay. This tidal bay is an outlet of Merrymeeting Bay and a drowned waterfall. It was drowned about 5,000 years ago. Before that, the Chops would have been a massive and awe-inspiring waterfall. Native American oral history still tells of this site's power. All six major Maine rivers drained through this one place. A narrow 600-yard-wide cleft is at the point where water flows out of Merrymeeting Bay and into the lower Kennebec River on its way to the ocean. The glacier carved this site about 10,000 years ago. The Native Americans called it Kebec, which means "spot that seemed closed," "closed in," "contracted," "plugged," or "that which looks closed." The prehistoric name for this area was Aquehadongonock, meaning "the portage area." There are lots of markings, or petrogylphs, in the area, probably telling of the dangerous passage. The word chops is an older name for "jaws." The Chops were the jaws where the bay closed below Merrymeeting Bay.

Waterfall Ratings

Topsham Falls

(Also known as Pejepscot Dam; Topsham Dam; Topsham Mill Dam; Great Falls of the Pejepscot; Upper Falls of the Pejepscot; Pejepscot Lower Falls; Pejepscot Falls)

Directions: I-95 to exit 103. Take I-295 to exit 31A. Take right to US 201, turn right onto Summer Street, then left onto Mill Street.

Amazing fishing took place on the Androscoggin River in Topsham in the 1600s. The Native American name Pejepscot means, "long rocky rapids part." These falls are located at the head of the tide and consisted of three pitches, with a total drop of forty-one feet. The upper pitch was eleven and a half feet, the middle pitch was fourteen feet, and the lower pitch was fifteen and a half feet. The middle pitch was nearly vertical. The natural falls formed over ledge composed of granite and gneiss. Ledge outcroppings extend from the water surface to points across the river, providing natural abutments for dams that have been superimposed at this site.

In 1673, the settlers took forty barrels of salmon and ninety kegs of sturgeon in three weeks from these falls. It was said at the time that if more salt were available to preserve the fish, more could have been taken. In 1869, two wooden dams were on the two lower pitches, but have since been breached. However, there is a dam at this site today.

Waterfall Ratings

Whiskeag Creek Dam
(Also known as Stevens Carrying Place)

 Directions: I-95 to exit 103. Take I-295 to exit 31A. Take US 1 N toward Cooks Corner. Take ME 209, left onto Centre Street, turn right onto Lincoln Street. Stay straight onto Oak Grove Avenue, which becomes Whiskeag Road.

This site is located on Whiskeag Creek in Bath. The name is Abenaki, meaning "creek runs near by dry at low tide." Historically, the Native Americans would come to this place, and then portage across the short piece of land here on the way to Merrymeeting Bay (The Chops). The short section was called Stevens Carrying Place. It was named for Thomas Stevens, who bought this land in the 1670s. The first mill was built here in 1753.

Waterfall Ratings

Somerset County

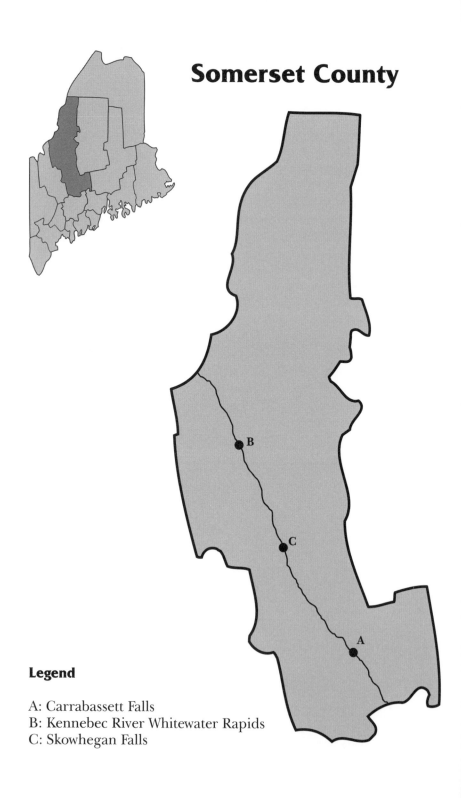

Legend

A: Carrabassett Falls
B: Kennebec River Whitewater Rapids
C: Skowhegan Falls

CHAPTER FOURTEEN
Somerset County

Sir Ferdinando Gorges named this county when he received a large land grant here in the 1600s. He lived in Somerset County in England and called his new land New Somesetshire. The King, however, wanted the area to be called Maine. Obviously, what the Royalty wanted won out, but Gorges perhaps won too. When Somerset County was created in 1809, it was named after the English County, just like Gorges wanted.

Baker Pond Falls

Directions: Route 2 South. Take ME 201 to Moxie Road. Turn left on Indian Pond Dam Road, right onto Brochu Road, left onto Bakers Road. There is a .2 mile walk to site.

These falls are located on the Baker Stream in the Caratunk area. The total vertical drop is thirty feet. At high water levels, in the spring or after rain, these falls become a "massive roaring descent of water." The falls have a distinctive appearance because steep gorge walls line the head of the falls, but the falls and the stream below are only slightly recessed from the banks. It appears that the falls are pouring out of a gorge rather than into one.

The bedrock is pelite and part of the Carrabassett Formation. The Carrabassett Formation comprises a thick sequence of graded beds of sandstone and dark shale. Mud rich sediments of the Carrabassett and Seboomook Formations flooded central and northern Maine in the early Devonian age. They are the precursor of the collision of the super continents Avalonia with Laurentia.

Waterfall Ratings

Bomazee Rips

(Also known as Bomazeen Rips)

Directions: Route 2 South. Take ME 201 to ME 201A to US 2. Turn right onto Upper Main Street, which becomes Winding Hill Road. There is a .1 mile hike from here.

These rips are on the Kennebec River in the South Norridgewock area. In 1724, the English killed the Native American Chief, Abomazine, and his child here in a surprise attack. They were trying to cross the river and were killed by bullets. The rips are named for him. The word in Abenaki means "keeper of the ceremonial fire."

Waterfall Ratings

Carrabassett Falls and Rapids

(Also known as North Anson Gorge Falls)

Directions: Route 2 South. Take ME 201 to ME 148 to ME 8 to ME 16.

Legends of the area claim that the revered Native American Carrabassett, the river was named for him, was murdered and killed in this gorge. These rapids occur where the Carrabassett River meets the Kennebec River. The water has worn away the slate rocks into peculiar forms.

There are several small cascade falls in this gorge, with a total drop of twenty-three feet. The gorge is a massive exposure of angular slate bedrock.

Waterfall Ratings

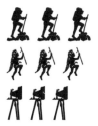

Carintunk Falls

(Also known as Caratunk Falls; Fall Brook Falls; Williams Dam; Thompsons Dam)

Directions: Route 2 South. Take ME 201 to ME 8 to Embden.

These were the most dreaded falls to lumbermen on Kennebec River in Solon and Embden. The five falls were almost a vertical 100-foot drop at one time. They were cascade and block falls. There are so many ledges in the area, which is one reason the falls were impassable and this was the "carrying place" to Native Americans. The word Carintunk is Native American meaning, "carrying place" or "forbidding or crooked stream." It could also mean "scrape field," because this is where the caribou would use their antlers to scrape snow away to find food in the winter.

The Native American relics and petroglyphs that have been found here date back 9,000 years. There are Native American petroglyphs found on a ledge two miles below the falls. These are thought to be Penobscot tribe glyphs; at one time this place was called Indian Ledge. In spite of these fierce falls, they were actually one of the easier falls for Benedict Arnold to travel than the three falls before (Norridgewock, Skowhegan, and Ticonic). It is also called the Old Canada Road site. In the 1800s, a drift net caught sixty salmon in one night at these falls. The Central Maine Power Company built this dam in 1939. In 1986, this site was added to the National Registry of Historic Places. The period of significance is 4999 B.C. to 1799 A.D.

Waterfall Ratings

Carrying Place Stream Falls

Directions: Route 2 South. Take ME 201 to ME 16. Turn right onto Ridge Road, turn right to Carry Pond Road.

These falls occur over a broad smooth ledge located on Carrying Place Stream in Carrying Place Township. The main falls appear as twin curtains of water, to the left and right, with a protrusion of exposed ledge between. The falls on the left constricts at the base, while the falls on the right fans out. This is a very photogenic fall site. The total drop is eight feet. This area can only be reached by following a logging road, where sometimes wash outs occur, so the falls are not always accessible by vehicle. The name of these falls is associated with their location along a principal carry used by the Native Americans to get from the section of the Dead River, an area now drowned by Flagstaff Lake, to the Kennebec River, an area now drowned by Wyman Lake. This carry meant that they didn't have to canoe the Lower Dead River with its many falls and rapids. It was also faster, saving miles of paddling, because the Lower Dead River heads north before reaching the Kennebec River near The Forks. Placer gold, andalusite, and staurolite have been found at this site.

The bedrock is Devonian-age granite. This age has been called the "age of fishes." This is the age when the exotic terrane called Avalonia collided with North America and formed the state of Maine.

Waterfall Ratings

Eel Weir Rips
(Also known as Pittsfield Dam)

Directions: I-95 to exit 157. Take ME 100 to High Street in Pittsfield.

These rapids are one of the oldest North American prehistoric fish weir places ever found. The dates that this area was used to catch fish are between 5,800 to 1,700 years ago. They are located on the Sebasticook River in the mouth of Alder Stream.

It is a well-known fact that in the early history of Maine, the Native Americans who inhabited the region used weirs to catch tons of fish in the short summer months. Weirs are wooden fences, usually crossed with brushwood, that are placed on the bottom of a river or lake to catch fish. A fish weir was created by using a set of wooden stakes secured into a river or lake bottom, attaching cross members and then weaving a web of brush through the uprights to form a latticework. A small opening is left, so fish and eels can swim upstream during the spawn. When the downstream migration starts, the opening is closed and the fish are trapped.

A weir could also be a dam that would force fish into a shallow pond, making it easier to catch them in nets or by spearing. There have been many weirs found in the ancient and now dried lake beds and river courses throughout New England.

In 1991, Sebasiticook Lake was being drained, and in this inlet, 600 stakes were exposed. These stakes were carbon dated, and showed that they were over 5,000 years old. There were two more artifacts found on the site, a half-channeled gouge and a large grooved cobble, which could have been a maul head or a net sinker. An unique object was found; a curled section of thick birch bark was sewn to form a container or basket. This craft was not known to exist during the time the fish weir existed.

Waterfall Ratings

Enchanted Falls

Directions: Route 2 South. Take ME 201, turn left on Piel Brook Street. Turn left on Transit Road, right on E Grace Pond Road, turn left on Shale Pit Road. (Parts of roads are unpaved).

The area received the name Enchanted because it was an apt description of the area, before the timber was cut, to early settlers. Here is actually a place called Enchanted Stream in Lower Enchanted Township where two falls drop. The lower falls are a five-foot vertical drop. The upstream falls are exceptional because the waters flows over black bedrock. The lower falls hide a cave in the rock. Caves are not common in Maine, so this is truly an unique and enchanted place. It is also part of the Seboomook Formation. Muscovite, Pyrite, Quartz, and Microcline have been found here. This was a major obstacle to log driving. Dams were once constructed upstream to enhance the flow during log drives, but they have been breached. High erosion on the east bank is the result of the dams in the area.

Waterfall Ratings

Gilman Stream Falls

(Also known as Gilman Stream Dam; Kingfield Dam Falls)

Directions: Route 2 South. Take ME 201 to ME 148 to ME 8 to ME 16. Turn left onto The Katie Crotch Road, turn right to ME 146.

This dam is located on Gilman Stream in New Portland/Kingfield area.

Waterfall Ratings

Grand Falls

Directions: I-95 to exit 244. Take ME 157 W to Katahdin Avenue to Bates Street to Millinocket Avenue to Golden Road. (Portions unpaved on all roads.)

These are classic horseshoe falls that have developed across the foliation of the bedrock located on the Dead River in Township 3, Range 4. This is an excellent example of this type of falls and is unusual in Maine, perhaps due to the fault line that runs across the river at this site. The foliation dips slightly upstream, which led to the undercutting that created the horseshoe lip. The water color is brown with a slight odor. There is a thirty-three foot vertical drop. There is an old wooden dam upstream that has been breached.

Waterfall Ratings

Holeb Falls

Directions: Route 2 South. Take ME 201 to ME 151 to ME 43. Turn right onto Eaton Corner Road, turn right onto Rowell Mountain Road, turn right onto Brighton Road, turn left onto Mahoney Hill Road. Turn right onto US 201, turn left onto Sandy Stream Road, turn left onto Gander Brook Road. There is a 1.1 mile hike from here.

Here is another natural phenomena that is hard to explain, but exists in Maine and can be found on the Moose River in Attean Township. This site is named for Holeb Nichols, who was an early trapper in the area. There are two parallel falls found here. The other is called Attean Falls. The main falls are a thirty-foot drop. The second falls lie southwest of the main falls and are parallel to each other. It is a portage area today, and unapproachable by vehicle. The bedrock is Attean Quartz Monzonite.

The Moose River in this area has an unusual anastomosing or braided pattern in the bedrock. The pattern is unique in Maine. This anastomosing pattern occurs only on sediment-laden rivers and is unusual for a stream in granite bedrock. Braiding occurs when a stream has numerous inter-twinning channels. This is often the result when a slope along the stream decreases or if the discharge of the stream decreases. The water color is brown, but has no odor. It has developed on granite with a blocky cleavage. These falls are the principal tourist attraction for the Moose Bow Trip. Brook trout is the species most often caught here.

Waterfall Ratings

Kennebec River Whitewater Rapids
(Also known as Kennebec River Gorge Whitewater Rapids)

Directions: I-95 to exit 157. Take Route 2 South to US 201 to the Kennebec River.

This is probably the best example of a geological youthful river flowing through the terrain. There is no other place like this in New England. These rapids can be found on the Kennebec River in Township 1, Range 7, and borders Piscataquis County. This is a steep ledge that drops within the first mile of a three and a half mile rapid. There are large standing waves that form over the riverbed during high volume. This site is basically inaccessible by road, and there is no trail along either rim. The rapids contain steep pitches and keeper holes. This area is in one of the longest and wildest gorges in the state.

The gorge is a V-shaped valley that extends for eleven miles. This is the only major section of whitewater that has been left and not dammed in the state. The water is odorless and light brown in color. It is an excellent habitat for brook trout and landlocked salmon. A few remnants of the log-driving days can still be found here. Canoes and kayaks use this area extensively. Today, it is part of the Maine National High Adventure Area.

Waterfall Ratings

Magic Falls

Directions: Take Route 2 South to US 201 to The Forks.

This wild water site is located on the Kennebec River in the West Forks area. It is used for white water adventures and has a twelve-foot drop. The pitch occurs over a large rock, called Magic Rock, in the Kennebec Gorge. There is a keeper hole just below these falls. Rafters know the rapids that exist on this river very well. These are rapids on the Kennebec River.

This is a "keeper" or a big hole, in the river that creates a huge standing wave. What are "keeper holes?" They are literally holes in the river. When a lot of water washes over a hidden boulder, it creates the hole. The river flows into the hole from all sides, making an area of water with so much air in it that a boat will not float. After falling into the hole, one also has to climb out of the hole. This is not an easy task. That is why the holes are known as "keepers" or "stoppers." This is a place where rafts have been known to flip completely over, throwing the rafters into the raging river. I know this experience personally as I was thrown from a raft while navigating this turbulent river at these falls.

Waterfall Ratings

Moxie Falls

Directions: Take Route 2 South to US 201 to The Forks.

These falls are actually one of highest single vertical drops in Maine and are located on Moxie Stream in Moxie Gore. Moxie is an

Abenaki word that means "dark water." The slate falls narrow to less than twenty feet, then plunge over a vertical sixty-foot cliff. There are several drops upstream, including a fifteen-foot perpendicular drop. The water color is slightly brown, but with no odor.

The bedrock is calcareous metasiltstone, which is part of the Hurricane Mountain Anticline and Dead River Syncline structure. Anticlines and Synclines usually occur in pairs. An anticline is an arch-shaped fold in rock where the rock layers are upwardly convex. The oldest rock layers form the core of the fold and outward layers are progressively younger rocks. Syncline is the opposite type of fold. The younger rocks form the core and have downwardly convex layers. This is a fishing spot for rainbow trout, brook trout, and landlocked salmon.

Waterfall Ratings

Moxie Falls. These falls are actually one of highest single vertical drops in Maine and are located on Moxie Stream in Moxie Gore. Moxie is an Abenaki word that means "dark water."

153

New Portland Falls

Directions: Route 2 South. Take ME 201 to ME 148 to ME 8 to ME 16. Turn left onto The Katie Crotch Road, turn right to ME 146.

This location on the Carrabassett River in New Portland is better classified as impassable rapids. The name comes from the settlers who came here after the Native Americans burned their homes in Portland. When they came to this new place, it became New Portland.

Waterfall Ratings

Norridgewock Falls
(Also known as Naulauehuwak Falls)

Directions: Route 2 South. Take ME 201 to ME 201A to ME 8.

These falls are located on the Kennebec River in Norridgewock. The name is Abenaki, meaning, "little falls and smooth water above and below." The name may also be in honor of the Abenaki Chieftain Norridgewog, who lived here. These falls drop over quartz rock and mica ledges, between ten to twelve feet for over a mile.

Benedict Arnold camped on an island nearby. Pipes and coins of that era can be found here. Benedict Arnold had to carry the boats around the falls. Things were just going to get worse for this troop before they reached Canada. At this spot, lack of food and illness were beginning to take their toll on his troops. This was a Native American camping site and portage area.

Old Roll Dam
(Also known as Old Dam)

Directions: I-95 to exit 157. Take ME 7 to ME 23 to ME 6 to Lily Bay Road. Turn left to Bear Brook Road to Greenville Road. Turn Right onto Loop Road. Turn left onto Poulin Road to Seboomook Dam Road (all roads have portions that are unpaved). There is a 1.2 mile walk to site.

This dam is located on the West Branch of the Penobscot River in Seboomook Township. The waterfalls here have nine total drops and are a portage site today. These are a series of upright tooth ledges made of green slate, which drop into the quick current and flat water. Each drop is about five to seven feet. Today, the water is slightly brown but has no odor. In 1884, the water here was described as a dark, reddish color with long bottom grass and weedy banks. Natural processes dictate that a lake will someday become a field. Eventually, the grass and weeds that grow on the bottom of the lake take it over completely.

The bedrock is green slate or phyllite with a forty-five-degree angle dip. This has led to the cuesta forms, which support the falls. A cuesta is the sloping layer of a landscape. If the angle of the slope is less than thirty degrees, a gently dipping layer that is erosion resistant will produce an asymmetric ridge called an escarpment or cuesta.

The falls name comes from a former location of a log-driving dam. This type of dam was where the logs rolled down to the water below after being floated up an inclined plane. There is no evidence of it here now. The logging companies made the Old Roll Dam using very simple tools. The old dams have been washed out or drowned by concrete dams. This is a fishing area for landlocked salmon with the average size being two pounds, but they have been caught up to five pounds.

Parlin Pond Falls

Directions: Route 2 South. Take ME 201 to Parlin Mountain Road. There is a .3 mile hike from road.

The rare plant, Arnica lanceolata, is found here on Parlin Stream in Parlin Stream Township. This an herb that is considered a globally rare plant. These are seventeen foot tiered waterfalls. They are a series of small drops developed over an orthogonal joint set. The water quality is excellent. The bedrock is either basalt or a hornfelsic quartzite.

There is an old logging dam and camp at this site. There have been logging relics found in the woods near these falls.

Waterfall Ratings

Sebasticook Falls

Directions: Route US 2. Take ME 152, turn left onto Commercial Street.

This drowned site was located on the Sebasticook River in Hartland. There is a dam here now, but the natural drop was thirty feet.

Seboomook Whitewater Rapids
(Also known as Seboomook Dam; Seboomook Falls; Henderson's Pitch; Grand Falls)

Directions: I-95 to exit 157. Take ME 7 to ME 23 to ME 6 to Lily Bay Road. Turn left to Bear Brook Road to Greenville Road. Turn right onto Loop Road. Turn left onto Poulin Road to Seboomook Dam Road (all roads have portions that are unpaved).

This place is an amazing and an extensive set of whitewater that contains steep pitches, chutes, large standing waves, and powerful eddies. These rapids are located on the South Branch of the Penobscot River in the Pittston Academy Grant Township, Township 2, Range 4. The name is Abenaki, meaning "at or near the large stream," or "small lake."

There are large boulders in the riverbed that have an unusual display of boudinage structures. Boudinage structures occur when rock units are deformed together with the most ductile units flowing and surrounding blocks of more brittle units. Deformation is very extreme here and well displayed. There are signs of differential weathering, too. The bedrock is green phyllite with interbedded quartzite and veins of milky quartz.

This area belonged to the Great Northern Paper Company during the logging era. Pittston Farm was located near here. This was an important lumbering camp during the log drives. It was also a Native American camping ground. This site is an important nursery for brook trout. The fish never leave the three-mile area where they spawn. There is an overgrown portage trail here, but this portion of the river is inaccessible. A fire warden's camp overlooks the most spectacular chute found on these rapids.

This dam was built in 1926, and was the largest wooden dam on the Penobscot River. The dam completely drowned a place called Hawk Island in about five feet of water. The island was about one mile long. After it was drowned, the island became a holding area with piers built on it. The name of the island is very old. It is thought that it was named for the fish hawk nests found in the dead trees all around the island. A logger named Henderson is said to have lost his life over these falls. The logging crew was so sure that they would be able to recover his body that they sent for a coffin. The body was never recovered and the coffin is said to have been set at the edge of the eddy pitch for twenty years. This was a very dangerous area. Tradition tells of many river runners losing their lives here while working.

Waterfall Ratings

Skowhegan Falls

(Also known as Great Eddy of the Kennebec River; Nine Mile Falls; Weston Dam)

 Directions: Route 2 South. Take ME 201, turn left onto Elm Street.

These were amazing and magnificent waterfalls located on the Kennebec River in Skowhegan at one time. Before the first dam was built on the island in 1790, there were actually two waterfalls. This site descended twenty-eight feet for over one half of a mile.

Also, there was a channel of water on the island known as "the sluiceway" that provided the prime spot to build mills and factories. It is no longer seen today, because the dams at this site have made the water rise. There was once a covered bridge here. A Town Lattuce Truss was built here in 1869 and removed in 1904.

A one cm nugget of gold was found here, and there are legends about massive rose quartz crystals having been found in the area. The falls offered great fishing for the Norridgewock tribe of the Abenaki, and the Native American word Skowhegan means "the place to watch for fish."

Benedict Arnold lost boats and men going up and over these falls on their way to Quebec City at the beginning of the American Revolution. In 1775, Arnold reported a vertical waterfall here, six times as tall as a man.

This was a very difficult carry. Not only did they have to go around these falls, they also had to go through three whirlpools and intense rapids before they even reached the falls. There is a bronze tablet on the island that marks their route.

The Central Maine Power Company built the modern dam in 1920. Today, a group is thinking of converting the gorge into a whitewater training facility for the United States Olympic team to practice.

When I visited this site, the roar of the falls, even with the dam calming the river, was loud and overpowering. It is easy to imagine what the first settlers must have seen and heard. The magic is still felt here.

Waterfall Ratings

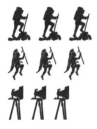

The Falls

(Also known as The Falls Rest Area)

Directions: Route 2 South. Take ME 201 until ends at Jackman.

This is a great place to visit. It is one of the few waterfall sites that the visitor can park near to visit. It is located on the East Branch of Sandy Stream in Sandy Bay Township and is a single, narrow, vertical drop of forty-five feet. The water splits around a ledge outcrop near the top and midway. The bedrock is fine-grained metasandtone of the Lower Devonian age.

Waterfall Ratings

Waldo County

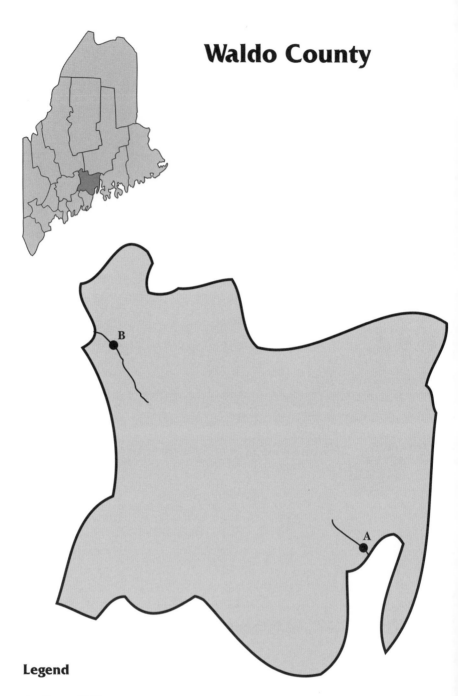

Legend

A: Great Falls
B: Monroe Falls

CHAPTER FIFTEEN

Waldo County

Beartrap Brook Falls

Directions: I-95 to exit 157. Take ME 100 to ME 220 to ME 9. Take left onto School Street.

The name comes from the fact that the first settlers saw black bear catching fish at the bottom of these falls Beartrap Brook in the Unity area.

Waterfall Ratings

Carlton Pond Dam

Directions: I-95 to exit 157. Take ME 100 to ME 220. Take left on unpaved road in Troy. There is a .1 mile walk to destination.

This dam is located on Carlton Brook, which creates Carlton Pond in Troy. This is an earthen dam, which backs up Carlton Brook, thus creating a protected waterfowl area since 1966. The original dam was a rock structure that was built in 1850 to provide waterpower for a mill that was located here.

Waterfall Ratings

Ducktrap Falls

Directions: I-95 to exit 161. Take ME 7 to US 1 to ME 173.

This fall site is located on the Ducktrap River in Lincolnville. They are cascade falls with no drop greater than two feet. It is a good spawning site for Atlantic Salmon. Sometimes the rapids in the village are also called Ducktrap Falls, but the fall site is about six miles upriver. The name comes from the fact that the Native Americans would trap ducks here, because when the ducks were molting, they could not fly.

Waterfall Ratings

Great Falls

Directions: I-95 to exit 157. Take ME 100 to ME 220 to ME 137 to Belfast.

This was a massive gorge and rapids on the Passagassawakeag River in Belfast with a dam at this site today.

It is well-known that the sea is an important part of Maine life. It is amazing that the ocean still has mysteries yet to be solved. Recently, a large number of pockmarks have been found on the seafloor of Belfast Bay, and are as large as football stadiums. They formed through the eruption of methane, a type of greenhouse gas that is trapped in the sediments of the bay floor.

The seafloor in Belfast is unusual. These formations are spread across a featureless muddy bottom. Most pockmarks are found over petroleum fields where methane gas forms from the high temperature breakdown of oil. It is believed that these pockmarks are not formed by oil, and the rocks in the region are metamorphic and igneous that formed at temperatures too high for oil to exist. The pockmarks appear to have formed recently from the production of methane in the mud around 10,000 years ago.

It has been stated that these pockmarks may be the largest in the world. The marks occur in a line hundreds of meters long and slope around twenty-seven degrees. The steepness and lack of infilling of the depressions at the mouth of the river suggest that gas escapes frequently, even today. The original source of how the geological formations occurred is still unknown. These formations are found worldwide.

Why is having pockmarks in Belfast Bay exciting, one may ask? There are six reasons:

1. Methane deposits represent immense accumulations of methane – more natural gas than geologists have found on continents.
2. Seabed pockmarks are thought to be formed when methane gas is explosively vented, perhaps when methane hydrate suddenly decomposes.
3. Offshore booms are often heard in areas where pockmarks are common.
4. Rich clusters of methane dependent life forms surround methane seeps.
5. The amount of buried organic matter required to create the offshore methane must be huge. Where did it all come from and how did it get buried at such depths?
6. Could the explosive decomposition of methane create giant bubble plumes that might engulf ships and cause them to sink like rocks?

Waterfall Ratings

Kingdom Falls
(Also known as Kingdom Bog Dam; The Kingdom; Muskingum)

 Directions: I-95 to exit 157. Take ME 100 to ME 220 to ME 9 to ME 3.

The ruined foundations of the seven mills that were built here can still be seen on the Outlet from Kingdom Bog, a tributary to the St. George River, northeast of the Montville area. It is a total vertical drop of twenty feet. The area is surrounded by thirteen-foot diameter White Pine trees. The falls developed across the foliation of the muscovite bedrock with lots of quartz veins in the area. There is also a three-foot wide pothole west of the falls. This was a Native American campsite in the Norumbega Backcountry.

Waterfall Ratings

Monroe Falls

 Directions: I-95 to exit 174. Take ME 69 to ME 139. There is a short .1 mile hike to the site.

This fall site is located on Marsh Stream in Monroe. The lip on the uppermost falls angle across the stream with a three-foot drop. The second set of falls is also a three-foot drop. The third set of falls is a two-foot drop, and the fourth set of falls is a three-foot drop. The slate at this site forms attractive patterns in the rock. There is also a fault at this site. The bedrock is calcareous sandstone. Hydraulic features are seen near the ledges. Ruins of the former mill, the walls only, are seen on the west bank of the stream.

Waterfall Ratings

Sennebec Dam

Directions: I-95 to exit 161. Take ME 7 to ME 131 to ME 3. There is a .1 mile walk to the dam.

Historically, the St. George River in Union supported Atlantic Salmon, alewife, blueback herring, American Eel and American Shad. The dam was originally constructed in 1916, as a 12-foot high and 200-foot wide dam. It was replaced with a rock fish ramp that recreates the natural riffles and pools needed to support the fish migration. The dam was removed in 2002. Removing the dam also significantly lowered a flooding problem that was causing concern in the area, as well as helped the fish population.

Waterfall Ratings

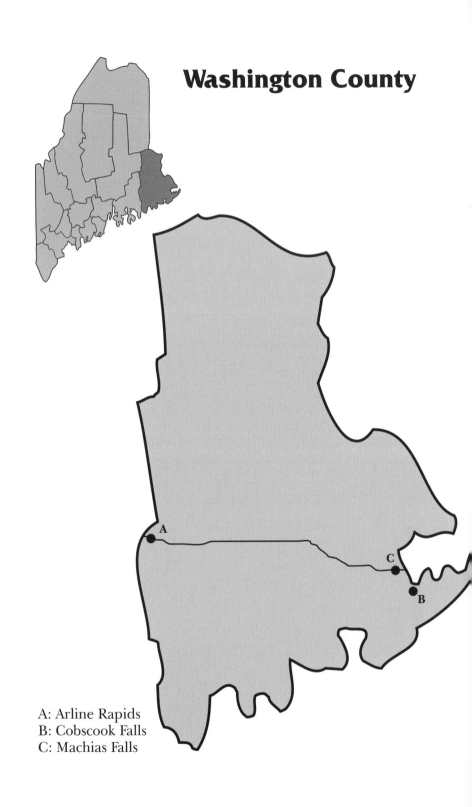

Washington County

A: Arline Rapids
B: Cobscook Falls
C: Machias Falls

CHAPTER SIXTEEN

Washington County

The St. Croix River is the largest watershed between the Penobscot and St. John River Valley. The system is Y-shaped because glacial and volcanic features run at right angles to each other here. Samuel de Champlain named the river because the Waweig River and St. Croix River form a cross where they meet.

Airline Rapids
(Also known as Route 9 Rips)

 Directions: I-95 to I -395, exit 182A. Take US 1.

This rapid area is on the Machias River in Township 31. It was a portage area or an ahwangan (carry out place) by the Abenaki tribes who lived here. In 1974, the dams on Third and Fourth Machias Lake were removed, so the Machias River is now a free flowing river. These rapids developed over a lag deposit of small boulders.

The larger boulders that were here were removed during the log-driving days to ease the passage of the lumber. The outcropping ledge here shows hydrologic sculpturing. This is an Atlantic Salmon nursery, and the water is clear and odorless.

The name comes from the highway that passes by it. "The Airline" or Route 9 was once used by airplane pilots as a visual reference point in the area that was heavily forested.

Waterfall Ratings

Canoose Rips

Directions: I-95 to exit 227. Take ME 6, turn right onto Bull Brook Road, turn right onto Loon Bay Road. There is a .6 mile hike to site.

Why would the Native Americans bury their dead near water or on the St. Croix River? There are still many questions about the Native American way of life before the Europeans arrived. This name is Abenaki, meaning, "graves there." Oral tradition states that a Native American burial site and/or graveyard is near this site, but nothing has been found yet.

Waterfall Ratings

Cobscook Falls
(Also known as Reversing Falls; Falls Island)

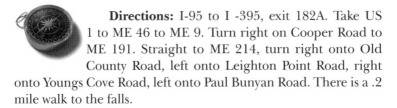

Directions: I-95 to I -395, exit 182A. Take US 1 to ME 46 to ME 9. Turn right on Cooper Road to ME 191. Straight to ME 214, turn right onto Old County Road, left onto Leighton Point Road, right onto Youngs Cove Road, left onto Paul Bunyan Road. There is a .2 mile walk to the falls.

These reversing falls are in a tidal channel in Trescott between Leighton Neck and Falls Island. They are located in West Pembroke in Cobscook Reversing Falls Park. The name is Malecite, meaning "rocks under water" or "boiling rock." The falls occur with the daily flow of the tides. Do not be fooled, however, if the tide is suppose to be low and the visitor is in the channel. A tidal surge could also occur because of storm winds or earthquakes.

The falls are really rapids that are caused by large boulders in a narrow passage of water. The boulders, in addition to the narrow passageway between the shores of the mainland and Falls Island, form a bottleneck that causes the rise in the depth of water on the neap side of the falls. There are actually two falls on the river. The falls flows about twenty-five-knots for about a half a mile. The sound these falls make drown out any other sound in the area. In 1990, this site was added to the National Registry of Historic Places. The period of significance is 499 B.C. to 1000 A.D.

Waterfall Ratings

Columbia Falls

Directions: I-95 to I -395, exit 182A. Take US 1. Turn right onto Epping Road, turn left onto Main Street in Columbia Falls.

These falls occur on the Pleasant River in Columbia Falls. This name comes from the word, Columbia, which is a synonym for America. They occur at the head of the tide. The natural falls are divided into two pitches with a total drop of fifteen feet.

Zoisite has been found here. This is a rock-forming mineral that is dark green in color. This area was settled in 1780 and well known as a ship building and lumbering center. This is also a protected Atlantic salmon fishing place.

Waterfall Ratings

Elbow Rips

Directions: I-95 to I -395, exit 182A. Take US 1 to St. Croix River.

These rips are located on the St. Croix River. The St. Croix River has the highest tides in the continental United States. The name of this site comes from the fact that these rapids occur on the "elbow" or bend in the river. The visitor can see four-foot pulpwood laying on the bottom of the river that is a direct result of log-driving days in the early 1900s.

Waterfall Ratings

Holmes Falls
(Also known as Lower Holmes Falls and Upper Holmes Falls)

Directions: I-95 to I -395, exit 182A. Take US 1 to ME 46 to ME 9 to ME 192. Turn right onto Bear Brook Road. There is a .4 mile difference from road to site.

The Machias River in Northfield falls are considered one of the most beautiful falls in Maine.The upper falls are a steep pitch of fifteen feet. The steep bedrock walls, more that fifteen feet high in places, line both sides of the river. The lower falls are considered a rapid developed over irregular jointed granite veins with basalt dikes and curved fracture structures. There are some steep pitches here, too. The total drop is thirteen feet.

There are many geologic features here that include, irregular jointing, irregular granite veins and basalt dikes, and curved fractured surfaces. A lumber road crosses the river shortly upstream from the falls. The bedrock is mafic with a diabasic texture. There is an Atlantic Salmon nursery here. This is a portage area today.

Waterfall Ratings

Leweys Rips
(Also known as Lake Rips)

Directions: I-95 to I -395, exit 182A. Take US 1 to ME 46 to ME 9 to US 1. Turn left onto Clapham Road.

This rapid site is located in Grand Lake Stream in the Princeton area. It is found near Leweys Lake, which is named for the Leweys family that lived here.

Also, on the Grand Lake Stream carrying place or portage in the area, there is an unmarked grave where a soldier, either American or British, was buried. It is said that the soldier was from the Revolutionary War era.

This entire place has a tremendous amount of water—more than twenty miles long and in some places five miles wide. It could be called one name, but because of the different narrows that connect the series of water, it has several names, which include Big Lake, Long Lake, Leweys Lake, and Grand Falls Lake. This site was continuous canoe passage in 1884, but dams have blocked the waterway.

Waterfall Ratings

Machias Falls
(Also known as Bad Little Falls; Machias Gorge; Getchell's Grist Mill)

Directions: I-95 to I -395, exit 182A. Take US 1 to Machias. Bad Little Falls park is between US 1 and ME 92. Visitors can park on ME92 side.

I have visited this place and the thundering sound found here is amazing. The location of the falls is six miles above the mouth of the Machias River. Machias comes from the Native American word, Mechises, meaning, "bad little falls" or "bad run of water." These falls are really a convergence of a huge waterfall feeding into the ocean or a tidal waterfall. The visitor can still see the logs lying along the side of the river from the log driving days.

This is a steep set of cascades around both sides of a rocky island that converge into a single water chute, then plunges into a long shallow gorge. It is a fifty-foot total drop and only a short distance from the ocean. There was a Long Truss covered bridge built here in 1842. The bedrock is mafic to felsic volcanic rock. Stories are told of the large amounts of Atlantic Salmon were taken from the bottom of these falls long ago.

Waterfall Ratings

Orange River Dam

Directions: I-95 to I -395, exit 182A. Take US 1. Turn left onto Playhouse Lane.

The name comes from the fact that the Orange River area was called Orangetown once. There is a concrete roll dam here at the site of an old hydro dam. This is the habitat of two rare birds; the Least Bittern and Bald Eagle.

Waterfall Ratings

Saco Falls

Directions: I-95 to exit 36. Take US 1S to exit 2A. Keep left at fork to Main Street. Turn left onto ME 9, take left onto Hills Beach Road. There is a .8 mile hike from here.

These falls are on the Pleasant River in Columbia Township. There are two high-volume drops of ten feet and a narrow flume found here. It is one of the most substantial falls in the northeastern region of Maine. The water is brownish, but odorless. The bedrock is volcanic rock. The remains of two abutments stand on either side of the river. There is also a fish ladder on the north side of the falls. This is considered a protected Atlantic Salmon site today.

Waterfall Ratings

Wigwam Rapids or Riffles

Directions: I-95 to I -395 - exit 182A. Take US 1 to ME 46 to ME 9 to ME 192. Take left onto Eastern Ridge Road, which becomes Two Lakes Drive. There is a .9 mile walk to the riffles.

This is a good example of a rapid formed over a lag deposit. It is one of the only rapids in Maine that cuts through a large glacial deposit of sand and gravel. There are three pitches and boulders twelve feet in diameter along the riverbed. These rapids are located on the Machias River in Township 25. It is said that the name comes from the Native American camp that was near here. It is a fact that Native Americans in Maine used the word wigwam to describe their conical huts covered with bark or mats. Another theory about the name is that it is Micmac, meaning "at the head," because it is near the head of the Machias River. Today, it is a nursery for Atlantic Salmon.

Waterfall Ratings

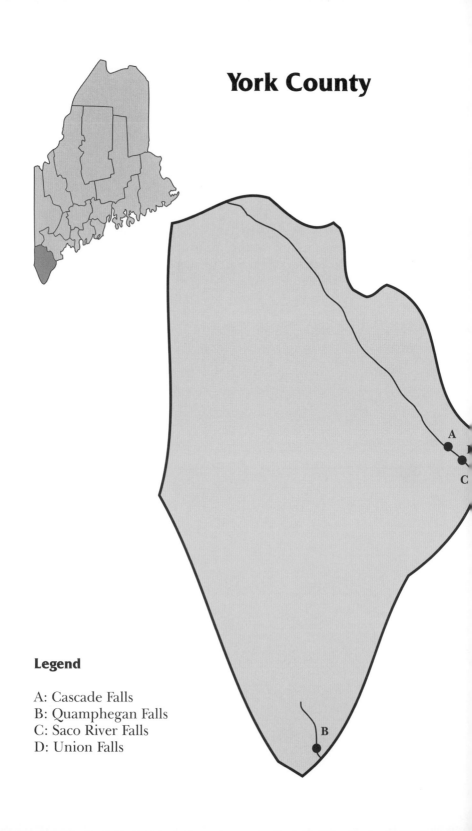

York County

Legend

A: Cascade Falls
B: Quamphegan Falls
C: Saco River Falls
D: Union Falls

CHAPTER SEVENTEEN

York County

The York River and all its tributaries are a spawning site for alewife. Bass and flounder have also been caught here. Even Atlantic Salmon has been fished in this area, but it is believed that the input of freshwater is probably not sufficient to support a spawning site for salmon, even historically. The Abenaki called this river Agamenticus, which means "the little river which hides behind an island in its mouth," or "other side of the little river."

Cascade Falls
(Also known as Bridal Cascade)

 Directions: I-95 to exit 36. Take US 1S to exit 2A. Take ME 5 to ME 112.

Many brides want beautiful pictures of their wedding day. What better place to have photos taken than at a waterfall? However, this site was called the Bridal Cascade because it looked like a bridal veil to a previous visitor. These are cascade falls found on Cascade Brook in the Saco area with a lengthy cascade down a rocky trough. The total drop is thirty feet. There are three falls here; the largest has a twenty-foot vertical drop. This was one of Maine's primary tourist attractions at one time. The old cage where State Wild Animal Farm in Gray used to bring a black bear to the falls each summer is still there. At one time, the falls were used to provide power for a water wheel driven mill. During the Civil War, slate was mined beside these falls and in the 1920s, a movie, *About Alaska* was filmed here.

The water is brown and contains some foam. There is also a large red pine standing here. This area appears to be an old sea cliff from the late Pleistocene time and graphically shows the amount of post-glacial rebound in this area. A dam was erected at this site to create a water storage pond. There has been at least one death from someone falling from the ledge into the falls.

 These falls are dangerous to climb and it is highly discouraged.

Hardscabble Falls
(Also known as Nasons Falls)

Directions: I-95 to exit 63. Take ME 115 to ME 25 to ME 11.

In spite of the name, this is an important whitewater rapid area. These falls are located on the Little Ossipee River in the Limington area, and drop sixty feet in a quarter of a mile.

This area is thought to be the initial retreat of a waterfall, which means that this is the interim stage between a waterfall and a meandering stream. The principal pitch is three feet falling at an inclined forty-five-degree angle. There are unusual hydrologic features here, which include eddies and exceptionally steep pitches. This is a portage site for canoes. The bedrock is granite and quartz monzonite. It is an important nursery for brook trout and the entire area is a wildlife sanctuary.

Waterfall Ratings

Hussey Plow Company Dam

Directions: I-95 to exit 19. Take ME 9 to Berwick.

This dam is located on the Great Works River in North Berwick. It has been a family business since 1835 to the present day. William Hussey built the dam in 1835 for his plow building mill. In the 1930s, the company realized that plows may not be the continued economic vitality that they needed to stay afloat, so they started to build seats for auditoriums and sports arenas.

Waterfall Ratings

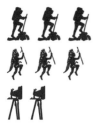

Kezar Falls
(Also known as Kezar Lake Dam)

 Directions: I-95 to exit 75. Take RE 202 to ME 122 to ME 26 to ME 117 to ME 35. Turn right onto Five Kezars Road.

These falls were on the Ossipee River in the Parsonfield area. The natural falls were really rapids that descended for fifty feet over a mile. The dam has drowned the falls here. This area was named for George Kezar, who hunted and trapped here in 1788. He also built the first footbridge over the falls. There was a covered bridge built in 1869. It was a constructed as a Paddleford Truss bridge.

Waterfall Ratings

Kezar Falls Gorge
(Also known as Kezar River Mill Dam)

 Directions: I-95 to exit 75. Take RE 202 to ME 122 to ME 26 to ME 117 to ME 35. Turn right onto Five Kezars Road.

These falls are located on the Kezar River in a winding gorge that is thirty feet deep and forty yards long. This is a twenty-five foot single drop in Lovell that terminates in a plunge pool. The water is slightly brown, but has no odor. The falls originated by the superposition of a debris-laden stream through stagnant glacial ice during the final phases of de-glaciation. The bedrock is muscovite granite.

The primary silver-bearing ore in Maine is Galena, and massive amounts of coarse crystal Galena has been found here. Galena is a common, lead ore mineral. Some Galena, however, may contain up to one percent of silver, instead of lead. Silver becomes a by-product of the lead production that makes Galena the leading ore of silver here. It is also a natural semi-conductor and was used years ago as the crystal of electronics. The color is silver gray, sometimes with a bluish tint. There are also claims that a true silver vein runs through this area.

Gold, Kaolinite, and Sphalerite have all been found here. Kaolinite is a glacial clay component. Sphalerite, which has been found in massive amounts, is a brown to black color. Sphalerite, which is also known as, Blende, is an important ore of zinc. Miners had a difficult time telling it from galena, acanthite and tetrahedrite, and all valuable minerals, so that it was named, Sphalerite, which is a Greek word meaning "treacherous rock," or the German word blend, meaning "blind or deceiving." This mineral's luster can actually be greater than a diamond's fire. It is a very attractive mineral. The color is black, but it can be brown, yellow, red, green, or even white or colorless. The other special attribute is that its cleavage is perfect in six directions to form dodecahdrons.

Spodumene, or tourmaline, has also been found here. There are stories that there is an old Native American lead mine near the falls. This is said to be one place where the Native Americans got their lead for knives and spears. It was also where they supposedly got the lead to sell to the colonists for their bullets.

Waterfall Ratings

Limington Rips

Directions: I-95 to exit 63. Take ME 115 to ME 35 to ME 25 to ME 11.

These rips are located on the Saco River in the Limington and Standish area. This is a good example of a rapid forming from the deposition of large boulders during the glacial era. Small potholes have formed here due to hydrologic action. Feldspar and Quartz crystals have been discovered here. This is also an important nursery for brook trout. There is a rest area at this site.

Waterfall Ratings

Little John Falls

Directions: I -95 to exit 19. Take ME 9 to ME 4 to ME 236. Turn left onto Scotts Avenue.

The United States Government actually destroyed this waterfall site. This is a place on the Salmon River that no longer exists. In 1828, the wading area and falls were dynamited by the federal government to make a channel for the gundalows to reach the mills at the Upper Landing, which is near the Counting House Museum in South Berwick. Beginning in the 1600s, Gundalows, flat bottomed, single-sail boats, were used to transport stores and supplies to gristmills, sawmills, settlers and others needing goods all along the rivers in Maine.

Waterfall Ratings

Moody Falls

Directions: I-95 exit 36. Take US 1 to Ogonquit.

These falls are only feet from the ocean which is very unusual. This place is located on the Ogonquit River in the Ogonquit area. It is a six-foot drop over a ledge. During high water volume, the falls divide into two columns around a protrusion of the ledge at the center.

Waterfall Ratings

Old Falls

(Also known as Great Falls; Flullen Falls; Pond Dam; Old Falls Dam)

 Directions: I-95 to exit 25. Take ME 35, turn right onto Alfred Road, left onto Old Falls Road.

Settlers actually had a head start about what to do with this part of the river, but today no one really wants much to do with it. This dreaded site is located on the Mousam River in Alfred. There is a natural stone dam that has created the falls. It has a forty-five foot total drop. The water color is bright green and has a bad odor; it is actually described as disgusting. The visibility in the water is only three feet. This water is among the worst in the state. There is also a man-made dam located at this site, near a fault that follows the river.

Waterfall Ratings

Pequawket Dam

 Directions: I-95 to exit 63. Take ME 115 to ME 35 to ME 25 to ME 11. Turn left Whispering Pines Drive, turn left onto Evergreen Circle, turn right onto Hangar Lane. There is a .3 mile hike to the dam.

Here lies one of the few known Native American historical spots. Located on the Saco River in Limington, it was part of a prehistoric trail called the Pequawket Trail. It was originally the main thoroughfare between the coast and the White Mountains. Native American oral tradition states that the Pequawket tribe made an annual trip from Fryeburg, which is the ancient home of the tribe, to the coast using this trail.

Quamphegan Falls

(Also known as Salmon Falls; Great Works Falls; Amoskeag Falls; Assbumbedock Falls; Auampheagan Falls; Tobaskick Falls; Great Falls; Rollinsford Dam; Salmon Falls Dam; Rocky Gorge)

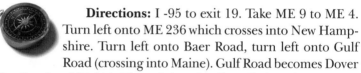

Directions: I -95 to exit 19. Take ME 9 to ME 4. Turn left onto ME 236 which crosses into New Hampshire. Turn left onto Baer Road, turn left onto Gulf Road (crossing into Maine). Gulf Road becomes Dover Eliot Road or ME 101. There is is a .2 mile walk from here.

The numerous names for this place tells the story of just how important this Salmon Falls River in South Berwick, immediately above the tidewater Piscataqua River, area was to prehistoric people, as well as to the settlers. The Native American names basically mean a "place of tall trees" and "place where fish is taken in nets" or "dip net falls." They are really more ripples or descents of one mile.

The Piscataqua River was called the Newichawannock, meaning "river with many falls" or "fork or confluence of two rivers" by the Native Americans. Native Americans used these falls to catch salmon and alewives in the spring. The rapids would suddenly appear when the tide was low. Legends state that the salmon leaping the falls here were wedged so closely together that a person could walk across the river on their backs. The Native Americans used two types of fishing here, weirs were placed in the tidewater Piscataqua River and the nets were used in the rapids of Quamphegan. After 1650, sawmills and gristmills were built on both sides of the river using the power of the falls, and the great fishing spot disappeared.

The name changed in 1650 to Great Works Falls because of mills there. The Great Works River was called Asbenbedick by Native Americans and was considered a healing and scared place to the Native Americans. Two ridges of ledge extending across the river formed the natural falls. The British set up a fort at these falls called Province Fort or Salmon Falls Fort from 1744 to 1755.

It was attacked five times by Native Americans in 1747 to 1755. That really does not surprise historians. This is just another waterfall site where the Native Americans and the Europeans settlers had a major conflict. Both sides were trying to find a way to survive in this harsh and unforgiving wilderness.

Waterfall Ratings

Saco River Falls
(Also known as Saco Falls; Little Falls Plantation; Biddeford Falls)

 Directions: I-95 to exit 36. Take US 1A to exit 2 to Main Street in Biddeford.

The creation of this dam is the single most important reason why Atlantic Salmon are no longer found in the Saco River in Biddeford. Located four miles from the mouth of the river, there are two main pitches to the falls; the upper one is eight feet high, and the lower one is a thirty-two foot drop. The river divides around an island just above the lower falls.

Native Americans knew it as a prehistoric fishing and hunting grounds. The first Europeans settled here in 1617, led by Richard Vines. They stayed one winter, and then left. Life was just too difficult here.

The British set up a fort at this site called Fort Saco. It was a British earthwork fort with a stone tower from 1693 to 1708. It was destroyed in 1843 due to factory or mill construction. A major textile industry was here in the mid 1880s. Here is another waterfall site where the two cultures clashed.

Waterfall Ratings

Directions: I-95 to exit 63. Take ME 115 to ME 35 to ME 25 to ME 11 to Limington.

One of the more easily accessible fall sites is located on the Saco River in Limington. There is a twenty-foot total drop and a walk to get to falls. These are block falls and considered one of the top volume falls in Maine. There is a Steep Falls Rest Area to leave the car for the journey to the falls. This is a protected Atlantic Salmon site today.

In the 1730s, Colonel Thomas Westbrook built a dam at these falls that interfered with the Wabanaki Chief Polin's fishing site of his tribe. Probably the Colonel built a dam over the natural waterfalls that ponded the water. Whatever the dam did, it stopped the fish from migrating during their natural migration, hence the tribe could not eat. So, Polin started to take revenge by attacking the settlers, but only after following the correct procedure and waiting almost seventeen years. Chief or Sagamore Polin complained that there were too many dams on the river to the Massachusetts Authorities, and that it stopped the fish from coming to these falls so the Native Americans were not getting enough food. This was in August 1739.

Ten years later, a new treaty between the Native Americans and Massachusetts was negotiated to remove the dams. Five years after that, the Native Americans and settlers started to fight about the removal of the dams. Two years after that, Polin was killed by the falls on May 14, 1756, as he led a war party against the settlers. He was said to have been shot by Stephan Manchester. It would appear that the clash between the Native American and European cultures came to an ultimate conclusion here.

Waterfall Ratings

Union Falls
(Also known as Union River Falls; Skeleton Station)

 Directions: I-95 to exit 32. Take ME 111, take left onto Summit Street, take right onto Round Hill Street.

The Native Americans named places to help them navigate this heavily forested state. This place is on the Saco River in Dayton. The French called this river Mount Desert, and the Abenaki called this river Wechkotetuk meaning, "comes out facing the falls at the head of navigation." Wechkotetuk can also mean "comes out river." The natural falls were seen when a Native American was traveling the river and came around a bend, suddenly facing the falls. They were impassable at that time, even by the excellent Native American birch bark canoes. The natural drop was twenty-six feet.

The name Union Falls is descriptive of where a small brook unites with the Saco River. These were considerable falls at one time, but now a Bangor Hydro dam called Skeleton Station has drowned them. The Saco River is a large river that has exceptional water quality. The British set up a fort at this site called the Saco Blockhouse in 1728. It was a palisade blockhouse and known to still exist in 1810. Beryl has also been found here.

There was a stone bridge at this site in 1869, and there was a covered bridge built in 1917. Another bridge up river was going to drown this site, and due to a public outcry, it was blown up as a stunt in a 1921 James Oliver Curwood movie that was being filmed here at the time. The steel trusses that still existed from that bridge were washed away in the 1936 flood.

Waterfall Ratings

Conclusion

There are many more fast water phenomena to be found in Maine. The sites listed give great examples of how the geology of Maine gave all our citizens life. From prehistory to today, these sites remain just a glimpse of the awesome power of nature.

Bibliography

Internet Sources

knox.link75.org
www.americanwhitewater.org
www.aria.database.com
www.avcnet.org/ne-do-ba
www.avcnet.org/ne-do-ba
www.avcog.org
www.bernardline.com
www.byways.org
www.campmaine.com
www.colby.edu
www.davistownmuseum.org
www.destinationmaine.com
www.ellsworthamerican.com
www.en.wikipedia.org
www.exploremaine.org
www.fishwier.org
www.fishwier.org
www.freepages.history.rootsweb.com
www.geostats.info
www.gorp.away.com
www.home.gwi.net
www.home.midmaine.com
www.kenebvalley.org
www.kennebvalley.org
www.knox.link75.org
www.lakesregioninformainegen.me.us
www.lat-long.com
www.livermorefallsmaine.org
www.loc.gov/rr/hispanic/portam/maine.html
www.maine.gov
www.maineflyfishing.com
www.mainenaturalarea.org
www.mainerec.com
www.mainerivers.org
www.mainetravel.net
www.mapquest.com
www.maxtrails.com

www.members.aol.com/flagman55/MaineMineralTourmaline
www.mineralgalleries.com
www.msad45.net
www.nationalregistryofhistoricalplaces.com
www.nationalregistryofhistoricalplaces.com
www.onedayhikes.com
www.outdoors.mainetoday.com
www.oxfordcountybicentennial.com
www.oxfordcountybicentennial.com
www.pearl.maine.edu
www.pittsfield.org
www.public.coe.edu
www.public.coe.edu
www.quoddyloop.com
www.swimmingholes.org
www.trails.com
www.visit-maine.com
www.wildlife.state.nh.us
www.wildsofmaine.com
www.wildsofmaine.com
www2.curtislibrary.com

Literature/Papers

History of Brunswick, Topsham, and Harpswell Part II, Chapter 9, "Diseases and Accidents," pg. 317, Augusta, Maine, Kennebec River Resource Management Plan, Maine State Planning Office, 1993

Kendall, W.C., "Bulletin of the United States Fish Commission, Notes on the Freshwater Fishes of Washington County," Augusta, Maine, 1884

Maine Historical Collections, 2, p. 273, "Kent' s Commentaries 3," p. 285, Wheaton' s International Law (Dana), p. 40

McMahon, Janet, "Maine' s Whitewater Rapids," Augusta, Maine, Executive Department Maine State Planning Office, 1972

Books

Bastin, Edson S. *Geology of the Pegmatite and Associated Rocks of Maine*, Washington, D.C., Washington Printing Office, 1911

Bates, M.L. *Abeanki The Dawn People*, Augusta, Maine, Gardiner Publishing, 1945

Blakemore, Jean. *Treasure Hunting in Maine*, Boothbay Harbor, Maine, The Smiling Cow, 1952

Bolnick, Bruce and Doreen. *Waterfalls of the White Mountains*, Woodstock, Vermont, Backcountry Publications, 1990

Bourgue, Bruce J. *Twelve Thousand Years American Indians in Maine*, Lincoln, Nebraska, University of Nebraska Press, 2001

Burr, Freeman F. Professor. *Gold in Maine*, Augusta, Maine, Maine State Planning Board, 1935

Cook, David S. *Above the Gravel Bar The Indian Canoe Routes of Maine*, Milo, Maine, Milo Printing Company, 1985

Eckstorm, Fannie Hardy. *Indian Place Names of the Penobscot Valley and the Maine Coast*, Orono, Maine, University of Maine Press, 1978

English, J.S. *Indian Legends of the White Mountains*, Boston, Massachusetts, Rand Avery Supply Company, 1915

Houston, Robert S. *Genetic Study of Some Pyrrhotite Deposits of Maine and New Brunswick*, Augusta, Maine, Department of Development of Industry and Commerce, 1956

Kendall, David L. *Glaciers and Granite A Guide to Maine' s Landscape and Geology*, Camden, Maine, Down East Books, 1987

Kingsbury, Henry D. and Deyo, Simeon L. *Illustrated History of Kennebec County, Maine*, New York, New York, H.W. Blake and Company, 1892

Levett, Christopher. *A Voyage into New England*, 1624

McCauley, Brian, *The Names of Maine How Maine Places got their names and what they mean*, Bar Harbor, Maine, Acadia Publishing, 2004

Nicolar, Joseph, Penobscot Tribe Elder. *The Life and Traditions of the Red Man*, 1893 based on oral traditions of the tribe

Snow, Dean R. *The Archaeology of New England*, New York, New York, Academic Press @1980

Stevens, C.J. *The Next Bend in the River - Gold Mining in Maine*, Philips, Maine, John Wade Company, 1989

Thoreau, Henry D. *The Maine Woods*, New York, New York, D. Appleton and Company, 1864

Varney, George J. *A Gazetteer of the State of Maine*, Boston, Massachusetts, B.B. Russell, 1886

Articles

Atikinson, Minnie. "Location of Township and some of its early history," Publication Hinckley Township or Grand Lake Stream Plantation, 1920

Babbitt, Bruce. "A River Runs through it America' s Evolving View of Dams," *Open Spaces Magazine*, 1999

Honey, Mark. "A Dockside View of Ellsworth, When Lumber was King," *Ellsworth American*, 2000

Kiley, Mack, Sharon. "Town watching dams decision," *Bangor Daily News*, 2001

Pike, Robert E. "Hell and High Water," *American Heritage Magazine*, 1967

Tarkinson, Dan. "The Presumpscot A New River," *Fly Fishing in Maine*, 2000

Tidd, Marshall M. "Up the Magalloway River in 1861 Part 1 and 2," *Appalachia Magazine*, 1957

There are numerous gorges to be found when exploring the Maine waterfall sites. The rushing water created this wonder and the falls that still exist in many of them are a wonder to behold and terrifying to encounter when on the water.

Index

Waterfalls are magical entities in their own right. The sheer volume of water, the thunderous sound, and the immense navigation obstacles are overwhelming when first observed. This water phenomenon staggers the mind of the observer, and it is really no wonder that these are usually considered spiritual and enchanting places of wonder.